Benjamin Godard, Edouard Blau

Dante

Lyrical drama in 4 acts

2

ROMANCE DU TENOR. Concluded.

Le Trouvère.

MANRIQUE.

Ah, que l'a - mour fi - dè - - le   touche ton cœur ma
Ah, let   a   faithful   love.................   touch   your   heart,   my

bel - - le   et re - con - nais l'ac - cent   du trou - ba dour pas
love.............   and   rec - og-nize the voice   of the troubadour passing

sant!   ah re - con - nais l'ac - cent.........   du trou - ba - dour pas - sant.
by,   and   rec - og-nize tho   voice.......   of the   trou - ba - dour passing.

Romance du Tenor. (Manrique.)

Andante.

Le Trouvère.

Piano. *ff*   *p*

MANRIQUE.

Ex-i-lé sur la ter - - re quand il gé-mit so-li
Ex-iled... on earth........... where a-lone he....

tai - - re é-cout-ez un-ins tant le trou-ba-dour chant-
sighs,........... lis-ten an in-stant to the trou-ba-dour sing-

ant é-cout ez un ins-tant....... le trou-ba-dour chant ant.
ing, lis-ten au in-stant....... to the trou-ba-dour sing-ing.

6

HAMLET. (Chanson Bachique) Concluded.

HAMLET. (Chanson Bachique.) Continued. 5

Le vin dis si pe la tris tes......... an
O wine, dis pel the sad ness..........

qui pè se sur mon cœur.......... à moi les rê ves de l'i
which weighs on my heart.......... to me the dreams of e -

orex so............ et le ri re mo queur! O li
brie ty........ ..... and the mock ing laugh! O en -

4   HAMLET (Chanson Bachique) Continued.

bas.................... so lour de chal - no era - els de-
world............. his heav y chain.................. cru el du-

poco rit

voirs, longs dés - es - pairs de l'âme hu - mai - ne.
tics. long de - spairs of the hu - man soul.................

f

Loin de nous noirs pré - sa
Far from us dark prog - nos -

ges, loin de nous noirs pré - sa - ges, les plus sa - ges sont les fous, Ah!..................
tics, far from us dark prog - nos tics, the wisest are the great - est fools, Ah!.... ....

f

un peu animé.

la   vie   est   som - - bre   les   ans   sont
Life....   is   dark....... ....   years   are

courts ....   de   nos   beaux jours........   Dieu   sait   le
short.... ....   of   our   bright days,........   God knows the

nom - bre..........   Cha - cun   hé - las............   porte   i - ci
num - ber,..........   Ev'ry - one,   a - las,............   carries in this

Hamlet.

Chanson Bachique.

I

Ô vin dis-si-pe la tris-tes.......... se
O wine dis-pel.... the sad-ness............

qui pè-se sur mon cœur.......... à moi les rê-ves de l'i-
which weighs on my heart:.......... To me the dreams of e-

vres se............ et le ri-re mo-queur, Ô li-
brie-ty............ and the mock-ing laugh,..... O en-

queur en-chan-te-res-se, ver-se l'i-vresse et l'ou-bli dans mon
chanting li-quor,.................. pour e-briety and oblivion in my

4   ROMANCE DE LA FAVORITE. ("Ange si pur.") Concluded.

En - vo - lez vous   Et   pour ja-mais, En   vo - lez vous, en - vo - lez
fly   far from me   and   for ev - er,   a - way,   for ev - er,

vous   et pour-ja - mais   loin   de mon cœur   ô   vous que j'ai -
for - ev - er,........ far   from   my heart, you   whom I loved,

mais,   En - vo - lez vous en - vo - lez   vous   et pour-ja - mais...............
....   a - way,   a - way   and for ev - er..................

ROMANCE DE LA FAVORITE.   ("Ange si pur.")   Continued.   3

Pressez.

á - me   Pi - tié   Sei-gneur rends moi l'ou-bli.   Pi - tié,   Pi - tié,........
my heart,   Mer - cy,   O Lord,   make me forget her. Mercy,   mer - cy,........

An - ge   si pur   que   dans un son - ge   J'ai   cru trouver
An - gel   so pure,   whom   in   a dream.   I   tho't I saw,

Vous   que j'aimais   A -   vec l'espoir   tris - te men son - ge
You   whom I loved,   with   my   hope,   sad   il - lu - sions,

2   ROMANCE DE LA FAVORITE. ("Ange si pur.") Continued.

En - vo - lez vous   et pour jamais   En - vo - lez vous.... Et pour jamais
Take your flight.   and for ev-er   Fly from me...... and for ev-er,

En   moi   par l'a-mour   d'une   fem - me   de
From   my   heart, the love   of a   wom - an,   had

Romance de la Favorite.

"Ange si pur."

DONIZETTI.

Larghetto.

An - ge si pur, que dans un son - ge j'ai cru trou-ver,
An - gel so pure, whom in a dream,..... I tho't I saw

Vous que j'ai-mais 'A - vec l'espoir tris - te men-son-ge
you whom I loved, With all hope's sad il - lu - sions,

2

LA BOHEMIENNE. Continued.

La Trovère.

pli - ce elle.................. est trai - né - e le
death she.................. is led,................ The

glas ré - son - ne El.......... du bu - cher...... cru - el
death-knoll rings,................ And of the stake........ cru - el

La flamme im - men - se...... s'è - lan - ce s'è - lan - ce au ciel......
The flames spar - kle..... and rise............ to the skies,.....

.... s'è - lance au ciel!
.... rise........ to the skies.

La Bohemienne. (Azucena.)

Le Trouvère.

La flam - me bril - le, Au -
The flames spar - kle a -

loin la fou - le ac - court sem - bla - ble
far, the mob............. runs............ like un - to

au - flot qui rou - le Pas - se u - ne fem -
a............. wave roll - ing. Pass - es a wom -

me hum - ble en - chain - né e Vers - le sup -
an hum - ble, in chains............. To a horrible

4

DANTE. (Romance) Continued.

Où le prin-temps met sa splen - deur............... A
All a-glow with the splen-dor of Spring;............. In

l'om - bre de ta re - nom - mé - e Une
the shade of your fame......................... An -

cresc. *f* *rall.*
au - tre ca - che - ra - - - son pai - si - ble bon -
other woman will live in quiet............... happiness............

heur............... O dou - leur!
O sufferings!

tranquille.

DANTE. (Romance) Continued. **3**

cresc.

Re - po - ser - ta pen - sé - e Ce n'est pas Vers les miens
mind in the eyes of the loved one, It will not be towards mine

cresc.

Que s'en i - ront les yeux. O cru - el - le dou -
that your eyes will turn. O cru - el......... suf -

ff

cresc.

leur!...........................
fering!...........................

dim.

pp

Comme un doux nid, sous la ra - mé-e,......................
As a downy nest in the fo - liage,......................

DANTE

give, but not see him says Beatrice. You might at least see some one else who accompanies him. Dante! exclaim Beatrice, and the two lovers are in each other arms.—Their rapture is infinite and they will never end. United at last they will live happy. But, alas! Beatrice's long sufferings have taken away all her strength and she falls dying in Dante's arms, repeating the w rds he hears her sin in his dream. She dies begging Dante to continue his divine poems, as the Muse of Poetry alone will console him Yes, must live yet, exclaims Dante, God has taken thee into His Eternity I shall make thee Immortal in my songs.

THE END.

2　　　　　DANTE. (Romance.) Continued.

tempo.

ra - - - son pai - si - ble bon - heur..............
.... in tran - quil hap-pi-ness..............

dim.　　　*rall.*

rall. < *f* > *p* *tempo.*

O cru - el - le dou - leur,..............
O cru - el........ suffering,..............

rall. < *f*

Quand tu vou - dras les
When, tired by your

p　　　*p*

sé - e Du la - beur glo - ri - eux En des re - gards ai - mants
glorious work.............. you wish to rest your wea - ry

pp

Tant de flamme
A l'instant que nous croyons
Enfermer tous ses rayons
Dans notre âme.
Ah! nous allons partir tous deux
Loin des hommes.
Partons.... Partons.

SCENE FINALE.

LES PRECEDETS, GEMMA, BARDI.

Elle fait quelques pas mais soudain elle tressaille et porte la main à son cœur comme si elle le sentait se briser. Elle chancelle, sa tête tombe sur l'épaule de Dante qui la soutient.

BEATRICE.
Ah! Dieu! Pardonne ami.
Je ne puis.

DANTE, *avec épouvante*.
Qu'est-ce donc? Cher ange!
Seigneur....
(*Silence de Béatrice évanouie. Gemma et Bardi accourent.*)
Venez.... voyez cette pâleur étrange,
Et ces yeux fermés à demi.

TOUS TROIS.
Béatrice entends-nous!

Béatrice revient peu à peu à elle.
BEATRICE, *à Dante.*
Le rêve était trop beau pour qu'ici bas
Le ciel permette qu'il s'achève... Je vais mourir,
Mais dans tes bras.

DANTE.
Mourir.... toi.... non.... je ne veux pas
Ma Béatrice.

Béatrice rappelant ses forces regarde autour d'elle, puis fait quelques pas vers la chapelle; elle joint ses mains, son visage prend une expression extatique, son regard est levé vers le ciel, elle semble déjà ne plus appartenir à la terre.

BEATRICE.
Je vais dans l'azur sans vo les,
Où les anges de leurs mains
Recueillent les pleurs humains
Pour les changer en étoiles.

DANTE, *se rappelant son rêve.*
La parole entendue aux célestes chemins.

BEATRICE, *d'une voix entrecoupée.*
Et nous serons unis.... Au radieux séjour,
Dans l'extase suprême et l'éternel amour.

DANTE, *sanglotant.*
Elle est morte.... ô mort.
Emporte aussi mon âme.

GEMMA, *à Dante.*
Hélas! ta blessure est cruelle,
Mais la muse est fidèle,
Et s'aura l'apaiser.

DANTE, *se redressant illuminé.*
Oui, je dois vivre encor,
Je dois chanter pour elle....
Dieu l'a faite immortelle,
Moi, je vais l'immortaliser.

Fin du Quatrième Acte et de l'Opéra.

So much flame,
At the instant when we believe
To look up at its rays
In our soul!
Ah! we shall both depart together,
Far from mankind.
Let us depart! Let us depart!

FINAL SCENE.

THE SAME, GEMMA, BARDI.

Beatrice walks some steps, but suddenly she shudders and places her hand on her heart as if she felt it break. She totters, her head falls on the shoulders of Dante, who supports her.

BEATRICE.
Ah, God! Pardon friend....
I cannot.

DANTE, *terrified.*
What is it? Dear angel, Lord.
Silence of Beatrice, who has fainted; Gemma and Bardi run to her.
Come—See this strange pallor,
And these half-closed eyes!

ALL THREE.
Beatrice, hear us!

Beatrice gradually recovers her senses.
BEATRICE, *to Dante.*
The dream was too beautiful, that here below,
Heaven would permit it to be accomplished....I
But in thy arms!   [am going to die

DANTE.
Die! thou....no, I cannot suffer it,
My Beatrice!

Beatrice, calling back her strength, looks around, then makes some steps towards the chapel; she joins her hands, her face assumes an ecstatic expression, her eyes are raised to heaven, she already looks as if no longer belonging to earth.

BEATRICE.
I go into the azure without sails
Where the angels with their hands
Collect the human tears
To change them into stars.

DANTE, *remembering his dream.*
The words I heard in the celestial regions!

BEATRICE, *in a broken voice.*
And we shall be united...in the radiant sojourn,
In supreme ecstasy and eternal love!

DANTE, *weeping.*
She is dead. Oh Death,
Carry off also my soul!

GEMMA, *to Dante.*
Alas! Thy wound is cruel,
But the Muse is faithful
And will know how to console thee.

DANTE, *rising, inspired.*
Yes, I must still live,
I must sing for her!
God has created her immortal!
I, I shall immortalise her.

End of Act IV and of the opera.

DANTE.

DANTE.	**DANTE.**
Béat~ico....	Beatrice.
Gemmo va au devant de Bardi qui est entré derrière Dante et tous deux se tiennent un peu à l'écart des deux amants.	*Gemma goes to meet Bardi who has entered behind Dante, and both remain at a little distance from the two lovers.*
BEATRICE.	**BEATRICE.**
Oh! mon Dante, c'est toi,	Oh my Dante, it is thee.
DANTE.	**DANTE.**
Ma Béatrice c'est moi. Tout à toi,	My Beatrice, it is me! All thine.
QUATUOR.	**QUATUOR.**
BEATRICE, DANTE.	**BEATRICE, DANTE.**
O l'ineffable et pure ivresse,	Oh the inexpressible and final joy
D'un cœur brisé toujours aimant.	Of a broken but always loving heart,
Je (le, la) revois, j'ai sa tendresse	I see (him, her) again, I have (his, her) love,
Soyez béni, Seigneur clément.	Be blessed, gracious Lord.
GEMMA.	**GEMMA.**
O l'ineffable et pure ivresse	Oh the inexpressible and pure joy
D'un cœur brisé toujours aimant;	Of a broken but always loving heart,
Voici la fin de sa détresse,	Here is the end of her distress,
Soyez béni, Seigneur clément.	Be blessed, gracious Lord.
BARDI.	**BARDI.**
Je les frappais dans leur tendresse	I struck them in their love
Par un indigne égarement	By an unworthy misdeed,
De mon remords vient leur ivresse....	My remorse has caused their joy,
Pardonnez-moi, Seigneur clément.	Pardon me, gracious Lord.
DANTE.	**DANTE.**
Ma bien aimée, il n'est plus rien qui nous sépare.	My loved one, nothing any longer separates us.
BEATRICE.	**BEATRICE.**
Que dis-tu?	What sayest thou?
Dante désigne Bardi que Béatrice n'a pas encore aperçu.	*Dante points to Bardi whom Beatrice has not yet seen.*
DANTE.	**DANTE.**
Celui qui fit le mal aujourd'hui le répare.	He who did the evil to-day repairs it.
Béatrice tend la main à Simeone qui y dépose un baiser sans pouvoir dire une parole, puis il s'éloigne avec Gemma, laissant seuls les deux amants.	*Beatrice gives her hand to Simeone who kisses it, without being able to say a word, and then goes out with Gemma, leaving the two lovers alone.*
SCENE V.	**SCENE V.**
DANTE, BEATRICE.	DANTE, BEATRICE.
DUETTO.	**DUETS.**
DANTE.	**DANTE.**
Nous allons partir tous deux.	We shall depart both together.
BEATRICE, *avec une joie craintive et presque enfantine.*	**BEATRICE,** *with a mixture of joy and fear.*
Partir tous deux....	Depart together.
DANTE.	**DANTE.**
Ainsi que des amoureux	Like lovers,
Que nous sommes.	As we are!
BEATRICE.	**BEATRICE.**
Partir tous deux....	Depart together....
DANTE.	**DANTE.**
Et bientôt sera trouvé	And soon will be found
Le cher asile rêvé	The asylum dreamed of
Loin des hommes.	Far from mankind.
BEATRICE, DANTE.	**BEATRICE, DANTE.**
Sans jamais nous effrayer,	Without ever fearing
Le monde peut nous railler,	The world may laugh at us,
Nous maudire.	Curse us!
Sur notre éternel aveu	For our eternal vow
Nous aurons du grand ciel bleu	We shall have of the great blue heaven,
Le sourire,	The smile,
Et notre unique souci	And our only care
Sera de lui voir ainsi	Will be to see it thus

SCENE III.
LES MEMES.

La porte du couvent s'ouvre de nouveau. Une religieuse paraît sur le seuil, Gemma l'aperçoit.

GEMMA, *à Béatrice.*

C'est moi que l'on appelle.

Gemma avec un dernier geste affectueux à Béatrice s'avance vers la religieuse, et, après un mot échangé à voix basse, disparaît avec elle. Béatrice regarde tristement Gemma s'éloigner.

BEATRICE.

Va compagne fidèle,
Tu n'as plus bien longtems à faire ton devoir.
Dante.... Mourir sans te revoir.
De l'éternel sommeil je n'ai pas l'épouvante.
Sous ta loi je m'incline, ô Seigneur triomphant,
Mais quand je mesouviens que je suis ta servante
Dois-tu donc oublier que je suis ton enfant....
Toi qui me séparais de celui que j'adore,
Rends-le moi pour un jour, une heure, un seul
                  [moment.
De mon dernier regard le contemplant encore.
Laisse-moi sur son cœur m'endormir doucement.
De l'éternel sommeil je n'ai pas l'épouvante.
Sous ta loi je m'incline, ô Seigneur triomphant.
Ah! si tu me gardais ces extases suprêmes,
Je m'en irais vers toi d'un vol si radieux,
Que tes anges eux-mêmes
En seraient éblouis dans la splendeur des cieux.

Avec découragement. Rêve insensé
Que mon sort s'accomplisse.... Dante,
Mourir sans te revoir.... ô Dante.

SCENE IV.
BEATRICE, GEMMA, puis DANTE, BARDI.

GEMMA *rentre en scène—à part.*

Je n'ose lui parler,
Sa faiblesse est si grande....

BEATRICE, *regardant Gemma.*

Qui peut à ce point te troubler?

GEMMA, *hésitant.*

Quelqu'un que tu connais.... demande
Si tu veux le recevoir.

BEATRICE.

Et qui donc?

GEMMA.

Simeone qui vient implorer ton pardon.

BEATRICE, *douloureusement.*

Ah! folle.... entre les folles
J'espérais un autre nom,
Pardonner... je le puis... mais le recevoir, non!

GEMMA.

Il n'est pas seul, et pour son compagnon,
Tu pourrais bien avoir de meilleures paroles.

BEATRICE.

Ah! Dieu.... Je n'ose croire.... et pourtant, ton
Ta main qui tremble dans la mienne, [émoi.
C'est lui.... C'est Dante.... qu'il vienne.

GEMMA.

Je t'en prie.... calme toi.

Dante paraît, s'élance vers Béatrice et la prend dans ses bras.

SCENE III.
THE SAME.

The convent gate opens again. A nun appears on the threshold. Gemma perceives her.

GEMMA, *to Beatrice.*

It is I who am called.

Gemma with a last affectionate sign to Beatrice advances towards the nun and after exchanging a word in a low voice goes out with her. Beatrice sadly sees Gemma go.

BEATRICE.

Go faithful companion
Thou hast not much longer to perform thy duty.
Dante.... To die without seeing thee again,
I do not fear eternal sleep
Under thy law I bow, oh triumphant Lord,
But when I remember that I am thy servant,
Shouldst thou forget that I am thy child,
Thou who separated me from him whom I adore,
Give him back to me for a day, an hour, only a
               [moment.
With my last look contemplating him still,
Let me gently fall asleep on his heart.
I do not fear eternal sleep;
To the law I bow, oh triumphant Lord,
Ah if then for me hast kept these supreme joy
I would go to thee so radiantly flying,
That thy angels themselves
Would admire in the splendor of the heavens.

(Discouraged.) Oh! foolish dream
Let my fate be accomplished.... Dante
To die without seeing thee again....oh Dante.

SCENE IV.
BEATRICE, GEMMA, afterwards DANTE, BARDI.

GEMMA, *returning, aside.*

I dare not speak to her,
Her weakness is so great.

BEATRICE, *looking at Gemma.*

What can trouble thee so much?

GEMMA, *hesitating.*

Somebody whom thou knowest....
Asks whether thou wilt receive him?

BEATRICE.

And who then?

GEMMA.

Simeone comes to implore his pardon.

BEATRICE, *sorrowfully.*

Ah, foolish one among the foolish, I nearly hoped
               [for another name.
To pardon....I can....but receive him, no!

GEMMA.

He is not alone and for his companion
Perhaps thou wouldst have better words

·BEATRICE.

Ah! God! I dare not believe....and still thy
Thy hand which trembles in mine,   [emotion.
It is him!....It is Dante....let him come!

GEMMA.

I pray thee....be calm.

Dante appears, rushes towards Beatrice and takes her in his arms.

Linceul des trésors à jamais perdus....
Assez de lys blancs sont ouverts dans l'ombre,
Qu'importe à l'autel une fleur de plus.
Le ciel ne saurait reprendre à son âme
Ce qui peut rester de bonheur humain
Pour moi ses regards ont si pure flamme
J'ai tant de douceur à presser sa main,
O toi qu'en secret sa douleur réclame,
Ange de la mort poursuis ton chemin!
Ne fais pas si tôt ses paupières closes,
Son beau front baigné de pleurs superflus.
Les champs de repos ont assez de roses,
Qu'importe à la tombe une fleur de plus.

Death cover of treasures forever lost!
There are enough white lilies open in the shade,
What matter to the Lord for one more flower.
Heaven cannot take from her soul
What may remain of human happiness
For me her eyes have so pure a flame,
I am so happy to press her hand!
Oh thou whom her sorrow in secret demands,
Angel of death pass on your way,
Do not have so soon her eyelids close,
Her beautiful forehead crowned with superfluous
The fields of repose have enough roses [flowers,
What matters to the tomb one flower more.

SCENE II.
Entre Béatrice.

BÉATRICE, GEMMA.
Gemma court au devant de Béatrice.

BÉATRICE.
Je viens te retrouver.

Gemma dirige Béatrice en la soutenant, vers le banc situé à droite.

Ta pauvre Béatrice
Ne saurait sans qu'elle faiblisse,
Demeurer bien longtemps à genoux....
Et le vœu
Qui devait me lier à Dieu
Est remis jusqu'au temps où je serai plus forte.

GEMMA, *essayant de sourire.*
C'est-à-dire à bientôt.

Béatrice se lève brusquement avec une expression d'effroi sur le visage comme si une vision sinistre apparaissait puis elle retombe sur le banc et sa figure reprend un air doux et résigné.

BÉATRICE.
Oui bientôt
Je serai tout à lui.... Mais là-haut.

GEMMA.
Ah, que tu me fais mal à parler de la sorte!
Ton cœur ne doit pas se fermer
A l'espoir des jours qui vont suivre,
Conserve encor désir de vivre,
Pour qui toujours saura t'aimer,
Non— ton cœur ne doit pas se fermer.

BÉATRICE.
Ah! C'est trop pleurer c'est trop souffrir
L'espoir, le courage en moi tout s'épuise
Mon âme agonise
Laisse-moi mourir,
Pourquoi me plaindre et t'alarmer
De nos maux la mort nous délivre
Mon cœur ne peut plus vivre
Puisqu'il n'a pas hélas! le droit d'aimer.
C'est trop pleurer.
C'est trop souffrir!
Ah! Gemma laisse-moi mourir.

GEMMA.
Oui, c'est trop souffrir,
Dieu prendra pitié,
Tu ne peux mourir.

SCENE II.
Enters Beatrice.

BEATRICE, GEMMA.
Gemma runs to meet Beatrice.

BEATRICE.
I come to meet thee again.

Gemma supports Beatrice to the bench on the right.

Thy poor Beatrice
Cannot without fainting.
Remain very long on her knees....
And the vow
Which was to give me to God
Is postponed until I shall be strong.

GEMMA, *trying to smile.*
Which will be soon.

Beatrice rises suddenly with an expression of terror on her face as if a sinister vision appeared to her; then she falls back on the bench and her figure resumes a gentle and resigned air.

BEATRICE.
Yes soon.
I shall be all his.... But above.

GEMMA.
Ah, how thou grievest me to speak thus,
Thy heart must not close
To the hope of the days which will follow,
Keep still the wish to live
For him who will always love thee,
No....thy heart must not close.

BEATRICE.
Ah! This is too much weeping and suffering,
Hope, courage, all are exhausted in me,
My soul is agonizing
Let me die.
Why complain and alarm thee,
Death delivers us from our sorrows,
My heart can no longer live
Since it has not, alas, the right to love,
This is too much weeping,
Too much to suffer,
Ah! Gemma let me die.

GEMMA.
Yes this is too much to suffer,
God will take pity,
Thou canst not die.

DANTE

come bearing palms and wreaths to decorate the poet's grave. One of them recites an ode to Virgil. When she retire at the fall day, Dante enters dressed in the historical costume. He is dreaming of Beatrice, whom he has not seen since his banishment, wonder are wether she loves or remembers him yet. Arriving near the poet's grave he invokes him and asks the Great Poet's shade to inspire him some divine poetry. The night has then come and the shade of Virgil is seen rising from the grave.

DANTE'S DREAM.

Virgil address Dante asleep and tells him, that human happiness is a thing very frail, his will break, but from his bleeding heart will arise the Divine inspiration. Night has come and from the back ground arises the vision of "Hell." Vague forms are seen, who cry in agony. From the multitude of them Dante distinguishes first the vision of Ugolin, who buried alive in the Tower of Hunger fed on the corps of his own sons; then appear Paola and Francesca da Rimini.—The horrible vision disappear and is replaced by that of Heaven.—Choruses of angels are heard, the scene is lighted by a divine splendor. In the midst of the splendor appears Beatrice. Dante recognizes her voice, she sings of the capture of angels and exhorts Dante to continue his task of Poet, which God will reward. The vision disappears.—Dante wakes up, and recalls his dream when appears Bardi who advances trembling to asks Dante's for giveness and tell him that he knows in what convent Beatrice is and that he has obtained from the church her release from her vow.

ACT IV.

The garden of a convent near Naples. On the left a chapel. On the right a stone bench, a door leading to the interior of the convent. Gemma seated on a bench deplores the sad fate of Beatrice, whom she sees dying; she hopes that her friend will not pronounce the final vows, but live to see her Dante again.—Nuns are seen coming from the chapel. In their ranks are Beatrice, who leaves them at seeing Gemma. Gemma tries to comfort her but Beatrice hopes that her martyr will soon end in death. At this moment some one calls out Gemma. Beatrice alone prays to God to take her away from this valley of tears, but to grant her see Dante before she dies. When Gemma returns Beatrice sees that she is much moved and asks her the reason. Some one wants to see you, and beg you forgive him, says Gemma, it is Simeone Bardi.—I can for-

DANTE.	DANTE.
Ah misérable !	Ah, miserable man!
Tant de tourments soufferts	So much torment suffered,
Et tant de pleurs versés,	So many tears shed,
Par tes remords seront-ils effacés.	Can they be effaced by thy remorse ?
La parole consolatrice	The consoling word
Aujourd'hui saurais-tu me la dire !	Canst thou tell it me to-day ?
BARDI.	BARDI.
Oui....	Yes.
DANTE.	DANTE.
Tu peux me rendre mes amours.... Ma Béatrice.	Thou canst restore my love, my Beatrice.
BARDI.	BARDI.
Je le puis, je le veux.	I can, I will !
DANTE.	DANTE.
Ah ciel !	Ah, heaven !
BARDI.	BARDI.
Gemma qui ne l'a pas une heure abandonnée	Gemma who has not left her for an hour
A ma pitié fit un suprême appel.	Has made a supreme appeal to my pity,
J'ignorais où la destinée	I knew not where destiny
Vous entrainait. Je l'appris.... Me voici.	Had carried you. I learned it....I am here.
DANTE.	DANTE.
Mais Béatrice où est-elle ?	But Beatrice, where is she ?
BARDI.	BARDI.
Près d'ici.	Near by.
DANTE.	DANTE.
A Naples ?	At Naples ?
Bardi fait un signe affirmatif.	*Bardi makes an affirmative sign.*
Ah ! Courons vite !	Ah ! Let us hasten ! [bidden.
Mais du lieu qui la tient l'entrée est interdite.	But entrance to the spot where she is is for-
BARDI.	BARDI.
J'ai confessé ma faute, et pour la réparer	I have confessed my fault, and to repair it
On m'a dans le couvent permis de pénétrer.	I have been permitted to enter the cloister.
DANTE.	DANTE.
Ah! viens, viens, courons vite.	Ah ! come, come, let us hasten.
BARDI, *l'arrêtant*.	BARDI, *stopping him*.
Vous me pardonnez	You forgive me?
DANTE.	DANTE.
Si je te dois l'ivresse	If I owe thee the happiness
De revoir encore sur les miens.	To see again on mine
Les yeux de la pure maîtresse	The eyes of my pure mistress,
Non tu n'es pas absous.... tu seras béni.	No thou art not absolved...thou shalt be blessed,
Viens.... Viens.	Come, come.
DEUXIÈME TABLEAU.	TABLEAU II.
A Naples. Le jardin d'un couvent. A gauche la	At Naples. The garden of a convent. To the
chapelle ; à droite, banc de pierre, et porte	left the chapel, to the right a stone bench
donnant sur les cours d'un couvent. Au le-	and a door leading to the courtyards of a
ver du rideau, les religieuses passent lente-	convent. As the curtain rises the nuns pass
ment deux par deux, se dirigeant vers la	slowly two and two towards the chapel.
chapelle. Gemma entre. Elle regarde le	Gemma enters. She looks at the passage of
défilés des nonnes en restant à l'écart. Béa-	the nuns while remaining on one side. Bea-
trice marche dans le cortège. Elle est très	trice walks in the procession. She is very
pâle et semble se soutenir avec peine.	pale and seems hardly able to stand up.
SCÈNE I.	SCÈNE I.
GEMMA	GEMMA.
Elle se rend à la chapelle	She goes in the chapel,
Ma pauvre amiée. En arrivant.	My poor friend....on arriving,
Chaque matin, dans ce couvent	Every morning, at this convent
Je me sens tressaillir d'une angoisse mortelle.	I feel a shudder of mortal anguish.
Au milieu de vous dans ce monastère,	In your midst in this monastery,
Filles du Seigneur ne l'accueillez pas	Daughters of the Lord do not accept her
Il faut, pour bénir le devoir austère,	To bless the austere duty there must be
Un cœur bien guéri des anciens combats.	A heart well cured of old combats,
A son cher amour ravi par la terre	Of her dear love, ravished by the earth
Elle songe encore en pleurant tout bas.	She still thinks while weeping in secret,
Loin d'elle écartez votre voile sombre	Keep far from her your somber veil

DANTE.
La voix de Béatrice aux célestes chemins.

CHŒUR DES ANGES.
Gloire à celui qui rayonne!

BÉATRICE.
Si la tâche n'est pas finie
Que doit remplir le bien-aimé,
Le Maître sera désarmé
Par sa constance et son génie
Et nous serons réunis au séjour d'adieux
D'allégresse infinie
Et d'éternel amour.

DANTE.
Béatrice! Entends-moi!

CHŒUR.
Gloire à celui qui rayonne.

La voix lumineuse s'éteint. Le rideau de nuages remonte, l'obscurité envahit de nouveau la scène.

DANTE.
Ah, plus rien! Dans l'espace....
Tout se tait! Tout s'efface,
Tout est noir
Oui! tu l'as dit Béatrice
Je pourrai te revoir.

Fin du troisième acte et du rêve de Dante.

DANTE.
The voice of Beatrice in the celestial paths.

CHORUS OF ANGELS.
Glory to him who shines!

BEATRICE.
If the task is not ended
That the loved one must accomplish,
The master will be disarmed
By his constancy and genious,
And we shall be reunited in the resplendent
Of infinite joyfulness   [realms.
And eternal love.

DANTE.
Beatrice, hear me!

CHORUS.
Glory to him who shines!

The luminous vision disappears. The curtain of clouds rises again and the scene resumes its obscurity.

DANTE.
Ah, no more! In space....
All is silent! All is effaced,
All is black!
Yes, thou hast said it Beatrice,
I may see thee again.

End of Act III and of Dante's Dream.

ACTE IV.

Même décore qu'à l'acte précédent. Au lever du rideau Dante est toujours endormi près du tombeau de Virgile. Le jour commence à venir.

CHŒUR DANS LA COULISSE. DANTE, BARDI, UN PATRE.

CHŒUR.

Ah!

Bardi paraît à droite. Un petit pâtre qui le précède lui désigne du doigt Dante, toujours endormi, et s'éloigne. Bardi fait quelques pas, puis s'arrête, n'osant l'aborder. Dante se réveille. Il promène d'abord un regard étonné autour de lui. Puis, se retournant, il se redresse et lève les yeux vers le ciel teint de rose.

DANTE.
Voici que l'aurore se lève,
Le brouillard matinal se dissipe dans l'air.
Soudain il se rappelle. Sa figure s'illumine.
Ah! le merveilleux rêve
Que j'ai fait.
Dante aperçoit Bardi et recule d'un pas.
Lui.... suis-je encore en enfer!

BARDI.
Pardonnez-moi... je suis indigne et coupable.
D'aveugle colère envahi
J'ai tout blessé, j'ai tout trahi....
Du courroux qui m'accable
Trop juste est la rigueur.
Pourtant, pardonnez-moi. Le repentir est entré
[dans mon cœur.

ACT IV.

Same scenery as in the preceeding act. As the curtain rises Dante still sleeps near Virgil's tomb. Day commences to break.

CHORUS BEHIND THE SCENES, DANTE, BARDI, A SHEPHERD.

CHORUS.

Ah!

Bardi appears on the right. A little shepherd boy who precedes him designates the sleeping Dante with his finger and departs. Bardi advances some steps and stops, not daring to accost him. Dante awakes. He first casts a surprised look around him. Then, turning around, he straightens himself and lifts his eyes to the roseate sky.

DANTE.
Aurora is rising,
The morning mist is dispelled in the air.
Suddenly he remembers. His face brightens.
Ah! The miraculous dream
I have had.
Dante perceives Bardi and recoils a step.
He! Am I still in hell?

BARDI.
Pardon me! I was unworthy and guilty
Carried away by blind anger,
I have wounded all, I have betrayed all!
Of the blame which crushes me,
The rigor is but too just,
Yet pardon me. Repentance has entered my
[heart.

DAMNÉS.
Ah!

VIRGILE.
C'est le tourbillon roulant sur nos têtes,
Meurtris, éperdus.
Ceux qui par la chair ont été perdus!
DAMNÉS.
Ah!...... Ah!
DANTE.
Ces cris de rage et de douleur....
Ah! maître défends-moi.... j'ai peur!
Virgile l'apaise du geste.
DAMNÉS.
Toujours.
DANTE.
Un souffle moins brûlant effleure mon visage.
APPARITION DE PAOLO ET FRANCESCA.
VIRGILE.
Deux êtres vont là-bas, se tenant embrassés,
Si pâles et si beaux qu'on dirait le passage
De colombes volant vers les nids délaissés
Et si tu veux savoir de quel nom sur la terre
On les nommait naguère
Et quel crime, en eux est puni,
Va demander à Rimini!

DANTE.
Paolo! Francesca! Dieu!
Une clameur déchirante d'angoisse et de douleur s'élève. Les cavernes sont incendiées par une immense lueur rouge. Un ange se dresse, tenant une torche flamboyante qu'il secoue sur les maudits.

DAMNÉS.
Pitié! Grâce! Le feu!
Fin de la première partie du rêve.
SECONDE PARTIE DU RÊVE DE DANTE.
LE CIEL.
DIVINES CLARTÉS.
VIRGILE.
Du gouffre où le maudit se tord sous l'anathème,
Que ton esprit s'envole au séjour bienheureux,
Séjour hélas fermé à ceux
Qui n'ont pas comme moi, reçu l'eau du [baptême.

DANTE.
Les merveilleux concerts.
Aux lèvres d'un mortel
Quel hymne jamais eût ces douceurs étranges?
La voix des anges; le ciel....
Je vois le ciel.
CHŒUR CÉLESTE.
Gloire à celui qui rayonne
D'ineffable splendeur.
Vous qu'il récompense ou pardonne,
Âmes des bienheureux allez vers le Seigneur.
Gloire au Dieu juste, au Dieu bon,
Gloire au Dieu sauveur.

APPARITION DE BÉATRICE.
BÉATRICE.
Je vais dans l'azure sans voiles,
Où les anges de leurs mains
Recueillent les pleurs humains
Pour les changer en étoiles.

DAMNED.
Ah!

VIRGIL.
It is the tempest rolling over our heads,
Crushed, desperate,
Those who by flesh have been lost.
DAMNED.
Ah! Ah!
DANTE.
These cries of rage and suffering.
Ah, master defend me.... I am afraid.
Virgil tranquillizes him by a sign.
DAMNED.
Forever!
DANTE.
A less burning breath brushes my face.
APPARITION OF PAOLO AND FRANCESCA.
VIRGIL.
Two beings walk down there, holding each other [embraced,
So pale and so beautiful, one would say the pas- [sage
Of doves flying to abandoned nests,
And if thou wilt know by what name while on [earth
They were call'ed,
And what crime is punished in them
Ask it at Rimini.

DANTE.
Paolo! Francesca! God!
A heartrending clamor of anguish and pain rises. The caverns are burned by an immense red light. An angel rises holding a flaming torch, while he shakes over the accursed.

DAMNED.
Pity! Pardon! The fire!
The angel with the burning sword!
End of the First Part of the Dream.
SECOND PART OF DANTE'S DREAM.
HEAVEN.
DIVINE LIGHT.
VIRGIL.
From the abyss where the accursed writhes un- [der the anathema,
Let thy spirit fly up to the realms of the blessed,
A sojourn, alas, closed to those
Who, like me, have not received the water of [baptism.

DANTE.
Miraculous Concerts!
From the lips of a mortal,
What hymn had ever such strange softness.
The voice of the angels, heaven—
I see heaven!
CELESTIAL CHORUS.
Glory to him who shines
With incomparable splendor!
You, whom he rewards or pardons,
Souls of the blessed, go to the Lord.
Glory to the just God! to the good God!
Glory to God the Savior!

APPARITION OF BEATRICE.
BEATRICE.
I go to the azure without sails,
Where the angels with their hands
Gather the human tears
To change them into stars.

Dante. (Romance.)

DANTE. (Cantilène.) Concluded.

cœurs......... *qu'un chant d'a - mour....* *et....d'es - pé - ran - ce* *de vrait mon-*
.... that songs of love..... and hope............. should a-

ter, mon-ter de tous les cœurs; *Le ciel...... est si bleu sur Flo-*
rise,........ from all..... hearts; The heavens are so blue above Flo-

rall. *tempo.* *Piu Lento.*

ren - ce qu'un chant d'a mour.... *et d'es - pé - ran - ce* *De-vrait mon-*
rence...... that songs of love..... and hope............. should a-

rall.

rall.

ter de tous les cœurs...............
rise from all...... hearts...............

16   DANTE.

VIRGILE.

Avant que de tes jours s'éteigne le flambeau,
Je veux que ton œuvre s'achève,
Et s'il est le plus sombre, il sera le plus beau.
Visite en ton sommeil, dont je guide le rêve
Le monde où l'on ne va qu'en sortant du tombeau.
Dante, je veux que ton œuvre s'achève.

LA NUIT.

Un rideau de nuages se lève lentement derrière eux.

DANTE.

La nuit ! L'horrible nuit !

Les nuages montent toujours. Il regarde dans le vide
avec une expression d'effroi.

Ces longs cris de souffrance....
Et ces mots que je vois tracés : " Vous qui venez
[ici,
Laissez toute espérance."

CHŒUR DES DAMNÉS.

Le rideau de nuages a continué son ascension et a
disparu. On aperçoit l'enfer. Cavernes som-
bres dont les routes ont par instants des effets
sanglants. Derrière des blocs de rochers noirs,
grouillent et se tordent des ombres confuses.

DES DAMNÉS.

Toujours.... Toujours....
O douleurs sans trêve ;
Châtiment sans recours.
Un cri s'élève
Des enfers sourds,
Maudits toujours.

DANTE.

L'enfer.... (avec terreur.) Non.... non....

Il cache son visage dans ses mains comme pour échap-
per au terrible spectacle.

DAMNÉS.

Ah....

VIRGILE.

Mon fils, poursuit ton rêve.

APPARITION D'UGOLIN.

DANTE.

Parmi ces malheureux,
Il en est un plus sombre et plus farouche.
Ah ! c'est affreux,
Du sang.... à ses mains.... à sa bouche.

VIRGILE.

Un supplice sans fin
Châtie un crime sans exemple.
Celui que l'on effroi contemple
Est l'homme qui mourut dans la tour de la faim.

DANTE.

VIRGIL.

Before the light of thy days shall be extinguished
I want thy work to be accomplished, [forever,
And if the darkest it shall be the most beautiful
Visit in thy sleep, the dream of which I guide,
The world where none go but after leaving their
[tombs.
Dante I will that thy work be accomplished.

NIGHT.

A curtain of clouds rises slowly behind them.

DANTE.

The night ! The horrible night !

The clouds continue to rise, he looks into space with
an expression of terror in his face.

These long cries of distress,
And these words I see traced. "You who come
[here leave hope behind."

CHORUS OF THE DAMNED.

The curtain of clouds continues its ascension and has
disappeared. Hell is seen. Darkness invades the
vaults which momentarily give bloody reflec-
tions. Behind the black rocks confused shades
roll and crawl.

DAMNED.

Always ! Always !
Oh pain without end,
Punishment without recourse.
A cry rises
From the deaf hells
Cursed forever.

DANTE.

Hell.... (with terror) No, no!

He hides his face in his hands as if to escape from the
horrible spectacle.

DAMNED.

Ah !

VIRGIL.

My son, pursue thy dream.

APPARITION OF UGOLIN.

DANTE.

Among these unfortunates,
There is one more somber and more troubled,
Ah ! This is awful,
Blood ... on his hands.... on his mouth.

VIRGIL.

A torture without end
Punishes a crime without example.
The one at whom thy terror looks,
Is the one who died in the Tower of Starvation,

DANTE.

LES ÉCOLIERS.
Ainsi que nous.... etc.
PASTEURS.
Honorons son repos.

*Les écoliers déposent leurs palmes sur le tombeau et
les pasteurs viennent à tour de rôle en s'inclinant
placer des fleurs et des épis.*

UN ÉCOLIER.
O maitre dont le nom ne peut être oublié.
Oui tou œuvre est notre Evangile.

TOUS LES ÉCOLIERS.
Dans un commun amour scellant notre amitié,
Nous restons frères en Virgile.

LE VIEILLARD.
Partous enfants, voici la fin du jour.

VIEILLARD et CHŒUR.
Voici la fin du jour.... etc.

Tous s'éloignent peu à peu.

SCÈNE V.

Dante apparaît, revêtu du costume historique.
Il s'avance sombre, la tête inclinée sur la
poitrine.   Le jour baisse de plus en plus.

DANTE.
Encore un jour qui tombe
Dans le gouffre infini.
Sans laisser un rayon sur le front du banni.
Où donc est Béatrice ? A l'heure où je succombe
N'a-t-elle pas perdu jusqu'à mon souvenir ?
Avec accablement.
Je suis si triste et las qu'il me faut une tombe
Pour qu'un peu de repos me puisse encor venir.
Il s'approche du tombeau.
O maître, leve-toi, dans l'ombre où je me penche,
Couronné de lauriers... Dans ta tunique blanche
Dicte-moi le poème idéal et rêvé:
Gloire et bonheur j'aurai tout retrouvé.
*Il va s'asseoir sur le rocher voisin de la tombe. La
nuit vient peu à peu.*

Folle chimère !
Mais je me sens accablé.... Ma paupière
S'abaisse.... un voile est sur mes yeux.
Ah! sois béni sommeil qui de la vie amère
Doit me faire oublieux.

LE RÊVE DU DANTE.—PREMIÈRE PARTIE

L'ENFER.

APPARITION DE VIRGILE.

*Dante s'endort.—La nuit est tout à fait revenue.—
Lentement la pierre du tombeau se soulève.—
Couronné de lauriers, vêtu d'une longue robe
blanche, Virgile apparaît, éclairé par un rayon
de lune.*

VIRGILE, parlant à Dante endormi.

Dante, c'est chose bien fragile
Que le bonheur humain
Le tien va se briser
Mais la Muse est fidèle et viendra t'apaiser.

*Dante a tressailli, il ouvre à demi les yeux, il aper-
çoit l'ombre et essaie de se lever. Mais l'ombre
étend la main et le poète retombe, ses yeux se fer-
ment de nouveau.*

DANTE.

Virgile!

STUDENTS.
Like us, etc.
SHEPHERDS.
Let us honor his repose.

*The students deposit the palms on the grave and the
shepherds one by one deposit flowers or ears of
corn.*

A STUDENT.
Oh master, whose name cannot be forgotten,
Yes, thy work is our gospel.

ALL THE STUDENTS.
In a common love sealing our friendship,
We remain brothers in Virgil.

OLD MAN.
Let us go, children. The close of day is here.

OLD MAN AND CHORUS.
The close of day is here, etc.
All go out gradually

SCENE V.

Dante appears, clothed in the historic costume.
He advances sad, the head inclined on his
breast.   The daylight disappears gradually.

DANTE.
Another day which falls
Into the infinite abyss
Without leaving a ray on the forehead of the
[banished one.
Where is Beatrice ? At the hour of my fall
Is she not lost even to my memory ?
With despair.
I am so sad and tired that I must find a tomb
to enjoy a little repose.
He advances to the tomb.
Oh master, rise, in the shadow in which I bow,
Crowned with laurels, in thy white tunic
Dictate to me the dreamed and ideal poem,
Glory and happiness, I shall have found all again.
*He sits down on the rock near the tomb. Night falls
gradually.*

Foolish fancy !
But I feel prostrated....My eyelids
Fall....a veil is over my eyes.
Ah! be blessed, sleep, which of bitter life
Makes me forgetful.

DANTE'S DREAM—FIRST PART.

HELL.

APPARITION OF VIRGIL.

*Dante falls asleep. It is fully night. Slowly the
gravestone is lifted. Laurel-crowned, clothed in
a long white robe, Virgil appears, illuminated
by a ray of the moon.*

VIRGIL, speaking to sleeping Dante.

Dante, it is a very brittle thing
Human happiness
Thine will be broken.
But the Muse is faithful and will come to console
[thee.

*Dante has shuddered, he half opens his eyes and per-
ceiving the shade tries to rise. But the shade ex-
tends his hands and the poet falls back, his eyes
closing again.*

DANTE.

Virgil !

J. A. SICARD,
BUILDER
144 GRAVIER STREET,
Bet. St. Charles and Camp.   NEW ORLEANS.

DANTE.
Adieu mes amours.
GUELFES et GIBELINS, BARDI.
C'en est fait.... etc.
Fin du Deuxième Acte.

DANTE.
Farewell my love.
GUELPHS AND GHIBELLINES, BARDI.
'Tis done, etc.
End of the Second Act.

ACTE III.

Le théâtre représente le tombeau de Virgile. Tout-à-fait à gauche du spectateur, un tombeau ombragé par de grands lauriers roses. Près du tombeau, un bloc de rocher couvert de mousse formant un siège. Au lever du rideau, groupes divers de l'asteurs et des femmes portant des gerbes de blé. Des jeunes gens et des jeunes filles dansent et forment un tableau très gracieux et très animé.

BALLET.
SCENE II.
UN VIEILLARD. CHŒUR.
LE VIEILLARD.
Partons, enfants. Déjà grandit sur la montagne
L'ombre du Pausilippe au déclin du soleil.
Voici la fin du jour, il est temps qu'on regagne
La chaume où nous attend le bienfaisant som-
[meil.
ENSEMBLE.
Voici la fin du jour.... etc.
LE VIEILLARD.
Par le sentier de la montagne
Je vois monter vers nous deux jeunes cavaliers.
Ce sont des écoliers
Qui viennent de la ville
Au tombeau de celui qu'ils appellent Virgile.
Entrent les écoliers qui portent des palmes et des couronnes. Ils vont se ranger de chaque côté de la tombe.

SCENE IV.
ODE A VIRGILE.
ECOLIERS, PAYSANS.
UN ECOLIER.
O maître, dont la gloire emplit tout l'univers,
Et dont la cendre ici repose,
La paisible demeure où nous bercent tes vers,
Demain pour nous doit être close.
LES ECOLIERS.
Demain pour nous doit être close.
UN ECOLIER.
Mais le temps plein de toi ne peut être oublié.
Et ton œuvre est notre Evangile.
Dans un commun accord, scellant notre amitié,
Nous restons frères en Virgile.
LES ECOLIERS.
Nous restons frères en Virgile.
UN ECOLIER.
O doux pasteurs,
Gardiennes des troupeaux,
Semeurs de la moisson dorée
Il disait vos labeurs
En sa langue sacrée,
Ainsi que nous honorez son repos.

ACT III.

The theatre represents the tomb of Virgil. To the left of the spectator, a tomb shaded by great red laurel trees. Near the grave, a rock covered with moss forming a seat. When the curtain rises divers groups of shepherds and women carrying sheafs of grain. Young men and girls dance and form an animated and pleasing tableau.

BALLET.

SCENE II.
AN OLD MAN. CHORUS.
OLD MAN.
Let us go, children,
Already lengthens on the mountain
The shade of Pausilippe as the sun sinks.
The close of day is here, it is time to return
To our huts, where beneficent sleep awaits us.
TOGETHER.
The close of day is here, etc.
OLD MAN.
By the mountain path
I see young cavaliers coming towards us.
They are students
Coming from the city
To the tomb of him they call Virgil.
The students enter carrying palms and crocus. They group themselves on either side of the tomb.

SCENE IV.
ODE TO VIRGIL.
STUDENTS, PEASANTS.
A STUDENT.
Oh, master, whose glory fills the universe,
And whose ashes here repose
The peaceful dwelling where thy verses inspired
Is to be closed to us to-morrow. [us,
STUDENTS.
Is to be closed to us to-morrow.
A STUDENT.
But the time spent with thee cannot be forgotten,
And thy work is our gospel,
In a common accord, sealing our friendship
We remain brothers in Virgil!
STUDENTS.
We remain brothers in Virgil.
A STUDENT.
Oh gentle shepherds,
Guardians of the herds,
Sowers of the golden harvests
He sang your labors
In his sacred tongue
Like us, honor his repose.

J'aurais vu leur ivresse insulter ma souffrance,
Et trahi sans pitié je les frappe à mon tour.

GUELFES et GIBELINS.
C'en est fait, il n'est plus notre maître d'un jour,
Sa grandeur est finie et la nôtre commence ;
Il perdra son orgueil en perdant son amour.

BARDI.
Maintenant vous pouvez remettre
Amis, votre épée au fourreau.
A Dante) Vous êtes libre, maître.
DANTE.
Ah ! fais donc jusqu'au bout ton métier de bour-
(aux partisans)   [reau.
Vous êtes insensés de me laisser la vie,
Ici je suis encore puissant,
Et de tout votre sang,
Infâmes, vous paierez sa tendresse ravie.
Rires ironiques des partisans.
CHŒUR.
Puissant encore tu le crois.   Ah.... Ah....
BARDI.
Entends-tu cette rumeur qui grandit et qui
                                   [monte ?
DANTE.
Qu'est-ce donc ?
Bardi s'est avancé à la croisée et a regardé dehors.
BARDI.
Charles de Vallois est entré dans Florence.
DANTE.
O l'effroyable honte....
*Nouvelles rumeurs plus fortes. Trompettes. Ac-
clamations.*
BARDI.
Ecoute encore, c'est son premier édit
Qu'on proclame et qu'on applaudit.
Trompettes.
LA VOIX DU HÉRAULT.
"Au nom du Roi de France, notre frère,
   Et par licence du Saint Père,
   Qui nous fait son représentant,
Nous, Charles de Valois enjoignons qu'à l'instant
Dante Alighieri soit banni de la ville.
Et ne puisse y rentrer sous peine de la mort."
DANTE.
Proscrit !   Je suis proscrit....
GUELFES et GIBELINS, *railleurs.*
Dès qu'on est le plus fort on exile,
C'est vous, Seigneur, qui nous l'avez appris.
DANTE.
Misérables....
*Béatrice est sortie de son accablement et chancelante
elle se dirige vers Dante.*
BEATRICE.
Dante....
*Les partisans tout en riant se retirent peu à peu au
fond de la salle en répétant le chœur.*
DANTE, à mi-voix à Béatrice.
            Tu l'as compris.
Par la force arrachée une promesse est vaine.
Si loin que le destin m'entraîne
Tu me suivras fidèle à nos amours.
BEATRICE.
Vous suivre.... J'ai juré, Dante, adieu pour
                                   [toujours.

Should I have seen their joy insult my sufferings
And, betrayed without pity, I strike them in my
                                   [turn.
GUELPHS AND GHIBELLINES.
'Tis done, he is no longer our master of a day,
His greatness is ended and ours commences,
Feeble heart, which foolishly dreamed of power;
He will lose his pride, losing his love.
BARDI.
Now you may return
Friends, your swords to their scabbards.
(To Dante.) You are free, master.
DANTE.
Oh ! Do to the end thy work executioner !
(To the Partisans.) You are insane to let me live,
Here I am still powerful
And with all your blood
Infamous men, you shall pay my lost love.
The partisans laugh ironically.
CHORUS.
Still powerful ! Thou believest it ! Ah ! Ah !
BARDI.
Doest hear this noise increasing and rising.

DANTE.
What is it then ?
Bardi advances to the window and looks out.
BARDI.
Charles de Valois has entered Florence.
DANTE.
Oh, the frightful shame.
New cries and acclamations, louder.

BARDI.
Listen still, it is his first edict
Which is proclaimed and applauded.
                                   Trumpets.
THE VOICE OF THE HERALD.
" In the name of the King of France, our brother,
   And by authority of the Holy See
   Who creates us his representative
We, Charles of Valois, enjoin that instantly
Dante Alighieri be banished from the city
Not to reenter it under pain of death !"
DANTE.
Proscribed, I am proscribed.
GUELPHS AND GHIBELLINES—*ironically.*
As soon as one is the strongest, one exiles,
It is you, my Lord, who have taught us that.
DANTE,
You curs !
Beatrice has recovered and staggers towards Dante.
BEATRICE.
Dante.
*The partisans, while laughing retire gradually to the
hall, repeating the chorus.*
DANTE—in a low voice to Beatrice.
Thou hast understood,
A promise wrung by force is null,
However far destiny may bring me
Thou wilt follow me, faithful to our love.
BEATRICE.
Follow you ! I have sworn ! Dante, farewell for-
                                   [ever !

DANTE

ACT II.

A hall in the palace, lighted by immense bay windows : in the back ground a rich tapestry hanging. Doors on both sides. Table and seats. Bardi, seated, is reading some documents. He deplores the measures taken by Dante in sending in exhile the leaders of the rival parties who have made appeal to Charles, brother of the king of France, but what incenses him more is that he has understood Beatrice's words and sees that she loves Dante. Enters Gemma who comes to beg Bardi to give back her word to Beatrice, who loves Dante since. Bardi declares that he will not give her up and shall win her love back. Rather give her up and pardon her, says Gemma,—You, then, do not know what is Love! says Bardi.—Gemma then confesses that she also suffers from unrequitted love, for she loves Dante, but knowing that Dante can be made happy only by Beatrice's love, she keeps her love secret. They depart and Beatrice who has heard all from behind the tapestry hangings enters. Like her friend Gemma she is ready to sacrifice her love to Dante's happiness, when the latter enters. She tells him that she is here to bid him a last adieu, but Dante declares that he cannot live without he, and that without the inspiration of her love his genius will die and he shall forsake poetry. Moved by so much love Beatrice falls in Dante's arms. In their extase they have not seen enter Bardi and the Gibelins leaders whom Dante has banished. They come to avenge themselves, and Bardi exacts from Beatrice that she shall give up Dante and swear to enter a convent or else she will see him slain before her. In spite of Dante's generous devotion in declaring that he would rather die than see her thus buried alive Beatrice swear to enter a convent, and Dante's life is spared but he is exiled in his turn as he had exiled the Gibelins. [Dante threaten to have them punished as soon as he is let free, but at the same moment are heard trumpets announcing the entrance of Charles of Valois in Florence, and heralds proclaim Dante's banishment.

ACT III.

The stage represents the grave of the poet Virgil, shaded by laurel trees in full bloom Near the grave is a moss-covered rock, used as a seat. At the rising of the curtain are seen gracefully grouped shepherds and women bearing sheaves of wheat. Young men and young girls, dance in groups and form a charming picture. They are about to leave the stage, when enter a group of students who

12   DANTE.

Le rideau se lève. Bardi se dresse devant Béatrice
qui pousse un cri de terreur.
  Lui....
    BARDI—Très froid.
N'appelez pas! Personne ne doit venir.
Il s'avance en scène.
  Ceux que vous réclamez
Sont avec nous ou bien sont désarmés.
    GUELFES ET GIBELINS.
  La résistance est inutile.
De ton palais et de la ville
Nous sommes maîtres aujourd'hui.
DANTE—Fièrement aux deux groupes ennemis qui
        l'ont entouré.
  Que demandez-vous donc ?
    BARDI—Aux partisans.
J'ai votre parole !
      TOUS.
  Oui.
Sur un signe de Bardi tous tirent leurs épées.
      DANTE.
  Assassins!
    BEATRICE—Affolée, à Bardi.
  Grâce, grâce pour lui.
      BARDI.
  Sa grâce est dans vos mains.
      BEATRICE.
  Que faut-il que je fasse !
    BARDI—Désignant Dante.
  Pour lui la mort......
  Ou pour vous le couvent.
      BEATRICE—DANTE.
  Le couvent.
      DANTE.
  Béatrice, que je meure
Plutôt que te pleurer vivant !
BARDI—Fait un signe aux partisans qui sont vers
        Dante.
  Alors....
      BEATRICE.
  Non, je vous en conjure....
      BARDI.
Jurez donc par le ciel implacable au parjure
De jeter à ce monde un éternel adieu,
Et n'étant plus à moi de n'être plus qu'à Dieu.
  Dante est toujours entouré par les épées.
      DANTE.
  Ne jure pas....
Bardi fait un nouveau signe aux partisans qui s'ap-
  prêtent à frapper Dante.
      BEATRICE.
  Par le ciel, je le jure....
      ENSEMBLE.
    DANTE et BEATRICE.
C'en est fait....séparés sans pitié, sans retour,
Nous avons devant nous l'éternelle souffrance...
Nos bonheurs, Dieu jaloux te sont-ils une offense,
Pour songer comme un crime à punir tant d'amour.
      BARDI.
C'en est fait, mon bonheur s'est enfui sans re-
                [tour,
Mais je suis sans remords. D'une juste vengeance

The curtain rises, Bardi appears before Beatrice who
utters a cry of terror.
  He! He!
    BARDI—very coldly.
Do not call. No one will come.
          He advances to the front.
  Those whom you would call
Are either with us or disarmed.
    GUELPHS AND GHIBELLINES.
  Resistance is useless,
Of thy palace of the city,
We are masters to-day.
DANTE—proudly to the two hostile groups who
        have surrounded him.
  What then do you want !
    BARDI—to the partisans
  I have your word !
      ALL.
  Yes.
At a sign from Bardi all draw their swords..
      DANTE.
  Assassins.
    BEATRICE—beside herself.
  Pardon, pardon for him.
      BARDI.
  His pardon is in your hands.
      BEATRICE.
  What must I do !
    BARDI—pointing at Dante.
  For him death....
  Or for you the cloister.
      BEATRICE—DANTE.
  The cloister.
      DANTE.
  Beatrice, let me die
Rather than to mourn thee living.
BARDI—gives a sign to the partisans who advance a
        step towards Dante.
  Then.
      BEATRICE.
  No, I beseech you.
      BARDI.
Swear then by heaven, unpardoning to perjury.
To say an eternal farewell to this man,
And being no longer mine to belong only to God.
  Dante is always surrounded by swords.
      DANTE.
  Do not swear.
Bardi repeats his sign to the partisans who prepare
  to strike Dante.
      BEATRICE.
  By heaven, I swear it.
      TOGETHER.
    DANTE AND BEATRICE.
'Tis done. Separated without pity or return,
We have before us eternal sufferings
Our happiness, jealous God, is it an offense to you
To punish so much love like a crime.
      BARDI.
'Tis done, my happiness has flown without re-
                [turn,
But I am without remorse of a just vengeance,

N'a droit qu'à ton oubli.
Ton époux, ton amant,
C'est moi, c'est moi seul.
    BEATRICE—*Tristement.*
            Poète, la gloire
Du bout de son aile, en votre mémoire
Effacera bientôt mon nom.
        DANTE.
    Non, Non,
Demain, si tu m'abandonnes
Pourrais-je encor chanter :
Je n'ai cherché des couronnes
Que pour te les apporter.
Sans toi mon œuvre est finie
Et n'aura duré qu'un jour.
C'est me prendre mon génie
Que me ravir mon amour.
    BEATRICE—*A part, avec extase.*
L'entendre ainsi parler, quelle ivresse profonde.
    DANTE—*Se rapprochant d'elle.*
Sur mon front l'orage gronde,
Chaque heure amène un danger ;
Il n'est que toi seule au monde,
Qui puisse m'encourager.
Ton âme aux douceurs célestes
De la mienne est la moitié ;
Par amour si tu ne restes,
Reste au moins par amitié.
        ENSEMBLE.
Tu le veux que mon sort à ton sort lié.
Je t'aime. Echos du premier jour
Jusqu'à l'heure suprême
Doit vivre notre amour;
Je suis à toi, je t'aime.
(*Elle se laisse aller dans les bras de Dante.*)

    SCENE V.—*Final.*
BEATRICE, DANTE, BARDI, VIERI, CHEFS
        GUELFES ET GIBELINS.
*La porte de gauche s'ouvre et sans être vus de Dante
et de Béatrice, perdus dans leur extase, entrent et
se trouvent debout sur le seuil Vieri et ses compa-
gnons.*
    CHEFS GIBELINS—*Railleurs.*
Cher Gonfalonier de Justice,
Daignez ici nous recevoir.
*Dante fait un mouvement pour emmener Béatrice,
mais Vieri et ses partisans lui barrent le passage et
le saluent ironiquement.*
        BARDI.
S'il vous plaisait qu'on nous banisse,
Il nous plaisait de vous revoir.
*Dante entraîne Béatrice vers la porte de droite, mais
il se trouve arrêté par Donato qui entre suivi de
ses partisans.*
    LES GIBELINS—*Railleurs.*
Illustre Prieur de Florence,
Nous réunir nous semble doux.
Mais seulement.... c'est contre vous.
        DANTE.
Quel traître vous ouvrit ce palais ?
    BEATRICE—*A part.*
Je frissonne....
(*Elle s'élance vers le fond de la salle en appelant*)
    A l'aide...... Au secours!

Has a right only to be forgotten!
Thy spouse, thy lover
It is I, I alone!
    BEATRICE, *Sadly.*
Poet, glory
With the tip of her wing in your memory
Will soon efface my name.
        DANTE.
    No! No!
To-morrow, if thou abandonest me
Could I sing again ?
I have sought for crowns
But to bring them to thee.
Without thee my work is ended
And will have lasted but one day.
It is robbing me of my genius
To rob me of thy love
    BEATRICE, *Aside, with enthusiasm.*
    What a joy!
To hear him speak so,
    DANTE, *approaching her.*
On my head the storm is gathering,
Every hour bring a danger,
Only thou in the world
Can encourage me!
Thy soul of heavenly sweetness
Is one half of mine!
If thou must not love me
At least remain from pity
        Pity
Thou willst it, let my fate to thine be linked
I love thee. Born of the first day
Until the supreme hour
Our love must live.
I am thine ! I love thee
    She falls into Dante arms

    SCENE V—*final*
BEATRICE, DANTE, BARDI, VIERI, GUELPH
        and GHIBELLINE CHIEFS
*The door to the left opens and without being seen by
Dante and Beatrice, lost in extasy, Vieri and his
companions enter and remain standing on the thres-
hold.*
    GHIBELLINE CHIEFS, *Ironically.*
Dear Gonfalonier of Justice,
Deign to receive us.
*Dante makes sign to lead Beatrice off, but Vieri and
his partisans prevent his passage, ironically salut-
ing him.*
        BARDI
It pleased you to banish us.
It pleases us to see you again
*Dante draws Beatrice to the door at the right, but is
stopped by Donato, who enters with his partisans.*
    THE GHIBELLINES, *ironically.*
Illustrious Prior of Florence
It seemed sweet to us to unite.
We have made this alliance,
But solely....against you !
        DANTE.
What traitor has opened to you this palace?
    BEATRICE, *aside.*
        I tremble.
She runs to the rear of the hall, crying :
        Help !....Help!....

Kuntz's Confectionery,

IMPORTER AND DEALER IN

FRENCH CONFECTIONERY,

CHOCOLATES, FRENCH FRUITS, FANCY BOXES, &c

Ice Cream and Lunch Saloon for Ladies,
AND RESTAURANT

No. 165 Canal St., New Orleans.

TELEPHONE 330.

ALBERT KUNTZ............Proprietor.

All orders for Weddings, Balls, Parties, Dinners, Suppers, &c., carefully attended to.

Restaurant opened until after the Opera.

MOËT & CHANDON

WHITE ★ SEAL

CHAMPAGNE

E. ✦ P. ✦ COTTRAUX,

WHOLESALE SOUTHERN AGENT,

140 .... GRAVIER STREET 140

Notre mal est adouci.
Un rayon doit encore luire
Dans l'ombre où je resterai,
Si j'entrevois le sourire
De ceux par qui j'ai pleuré.
Apaisez votre colère,
Et pardonnez noblement;
Comme vous je désespère,
Comme moi soyez clément.

BARDI.
Folle et lâche femme.
Pardonner la douleur
Est facile a ton âme,
Mais je n'ai que la haine et la vengeance au
Oui, je veux me venger.   [cœur.

GEMMA—BARDI.
Pitié pour eux, pitié seigneur, etc.,
Folle et lâche femme, etc.   (*Ils sortent.*)

SCENE III.
La tapisserie du fond s'écarte, Béatrice apparaît.

BEATRICE.
Paroles de haine, aveu de tendresse,
J'ai tout entendu.
Pour tous je saurais tenir ma promesse ;
Mon dernier espoir, cher Dante, est perdu.

AIR.
Comme un doux nid sous la ramée,
A l'ombre de ta renommée
Une autre cachera son paisible bonheur.
O cruelle douleur!
Quand tu voudras, lassée
Du labeur glorieux,
En des regards aimants reposer ta pensée,
Ce n'est pas vers les miens que s'en iront tes
O cruelle douleur !   [yeux.
Comme un doux nid sous la ramée
Où le printemps met sa splendeur,
A l'ombre de ta renommée,
Un autre cachera son paisible bonheur.
Ah! que la mort soit prompte à délivrer mes
peines.

SCENE IV.
BEATRICE. DANTE.
En ce moment Dante, ouvrant la porte de gauche, s'avance le front baissé, et sans apercevoir d'abord Béatrice qui tressaille douloureusement à sa vue.

BEATRICE.
C'est lui, Seigneur, en ce cruel instant soutenez-
DANTE—*Apercevant Béatrice.*   [moi.
Béatrice! Après tant de messages et de prières
vaines.
Enfin, c'est vous que je revois.

BEATTICE.
Dante, vous me voyez pour la dernière fois.

DANTE.
Sur ta lèvre est l'adieu
Et non dans ta pensée.

BEATRICE.
Je suis la fiancée
D'un homme à qui je dois
Un de mes jours heureux,
Et je n'en compte guère,

DANTE.
Ah! celui qui naguère
De ta douleur abusait lâchement

Our pain is alleviated
A ray shall yet pierce
Into the shadow, where I shall remain
If I see the smile
Of those for whom I have wept.
Abate your anger
And nobly pardon!
Like you I dispair
Like me be forgiving

BARDI.
Foolish and cowardly woman!
To pardon the pain
Is easy to thy soul
But I have only hate and vengeance in my heart!
Yes I want revenge.

GEMMA
Pity for them, my God, etc.

BARDI.
Foolish and coward woman, etc. *They go out.*

SCENE III
The tapestry in the rear opens, Beatrice appears.

BEATRICE
Words of hate I avowal of love
I heard it all !
For all I shall know to keep my promise.
My last hope, dear Dante, is lost.

AIR
Like a sweet nest under the foliage
In the shadow of thy fame
Another will hide her peaceful happiness.
Oh cruel pain!
When thou willst, tired
Of glorious labors.
Repose thy thought In loving eyes.
Thine eyes will not look towards mine
Oh cruel pain.
Like a sweet nest under the foliage
Where spring puts its splendor
In the shadow of thy fame
Another will hide her peaceful happiness.
Ah! may death be quick to deliver me from my
(sorrow

SCENE IV
BEATRICE, DANTE
At this moment Dante, opening the door to the left, advances with bowed head, without at first perceiving Beatrice, who trembles painfully on seeing him

BEATRICE.
It is him, Lord! At this cruel instant sustain me.
DANTE, *(perceiving Beatrice)*
After so many messages and vain prayers
At last I see you again!

BEATRICE.
Dante, you see me for the last time

DANTE
In thy words is the farewell
But not in thy thought.

BEATRICE
I am the betrothed
Of a man to whom I owe
One of my happy days.
And I do not count many of them!

DANTE.
Ah! He who then
Vilely took advantage of thy sorrow

Ce n'est pas seulement sur nous que tout est noir. Ah! c'est en moi. Ces mots, ces mots, je les entends sans cesse: "Va sans regrets, sois sans faiblesse, Pour être aimé fais ton devoir. Quelle flamme alors j'ai cru voir dans ses yeux. Non! à trahir sa promesse Elle n'a pu songer. Et je n'ai pas encore d'abandon à venger. Qu'on ouvre à l'étranger les portes de Florence. O maître, et c'en est fait d'un reste de pouvoir. *(Il s'assied de nouveau et continue à parcourir les papiers qui sont sur la table.)*	It is not alone for us that all looks dark, Ah! In me, too, Those words, these words, I ever hear them: "Go without regret, be without weakness, To be loved, do thy duty." What a flame I thought to see in her eyes· No! to betray her promise, She could not have thought of it. And I have not yet her abandonment to revenge. Let the gates of Florence be open to the strangers, Oh! masters, and that ends the remains of your [power. *He sits himself again and continues to peruse the papers on the table.*
SCENE II.	**SCENE II.**
GEMMA. BARDI. *(Gemma entre par la droite.)* BARDI. *(Allant vivement vers Gemma.)* Gemma! La chère Béatrice. A-t-elle enfin fixé le jour de notre hymen ? GEMMA. Je viens vous demander un cruel sacrifice. *(Tressaillement de Bardi.)* Mais digne d'un grand cœur. Renoncez à sa main. BARDI. Je l'attendais cette parole, Ma tendresse n'est pas si folle Qu'elle n'ait vu la trahison. GEMMA. Ah! vous accusez sans raison; Béatrice à cette heure Ignore ce que je fais mais elle pleure, Et je revois son front plus pâle chaque jour. Oubliez sa promesse. BARDI. Oublier cet amour. *Il se rapproche de Gemma et lui parle avec une rage contenue.* Oui, si je la délie, Dès que j'aurai parlé, Sur sa lèvre palie Je sais que reviendra le sourire envolé. Oui, ses yeux dont les charmes Ont pris mon faible cœur, Si je taris ses larmes, Retrouveront bientôt leur première douceur. Mais tu l'as bien compris docile messagère, Alors, nous la verrons radieuse et légère, Courir à son amant et tomber dans ses bras. *(sourdement)* Et cet amant, c'est Dante, n'est-ce pas ?	GEMMA, BARDI. *(Gemma enters from the right.)* BARDI—*Going towards Gemma.* Gemma. Has the dear Beatrice At last appointed the day for our nuptial ? GEMMA. I come to ask you a cruel sacrifice. *(Bardi is violently moved.)* But worthy of a great heart. Renounce her hand BARDI. I expected this word ! My tenderness is not so insane. That it has not seen the treason! GEMMA. Ah! You accuse without reason! Beatrice at this hour Is ignorant of what I do, but she weeps, And I see her face growing paler every day Forget her promise! BARDI. Forget this love! *He approaches Gemma and speaks with contained rage.* Yes, If I release her, As soon as I shall have spoken On her paled lips The last smile will return. Yes, her eyes whose charms Have conquered my weak heart. If I dry their tears, Will soon recover their pristine sweetness ! But thou hast well understood it, faithful messen- [ger, Then we shall see her radiant and light hearted, Running to her lover and falling into his arms. *(angrily.)* And this lover, it is Dante, is it not [so ?
GEMMA. A lui, dès son enfance, elle s'était donnée, Et ne pouvait le revoir sans émoi. Par vous qu'elle soit pardonnée. BARDI. Pardonner! On voit bien que tu n'aimes pas. GEMMA. Hélas? mon âme est blessée Comme la vôtre J'ai le même tourment, Et c'est Dante que j'aime. BARDI. Et tu veux insensée Jeter ma Beatrice aux bras de ton amant. GEMMA.—*Avec une expression très douce.* Si ma douleur est amère, Pourtant, je le sais aussi Par le bien que l'on peut faire,	GEMMA. To him she gave her heart in her childhood, And could not see him again without emotion. Then let her be pardoned by you ! BARDI. To pardon! Oh one can see that thou lovest not. GEMMA. Alas! My soul is wounded, Like yours, I have the same torment And it is Dante whom I love. BARDI. And thou wantest me to madly Throw my Beatrice into the arms of thy lover. GEMMA.—*With a very soft expression.* If my pain is gretter, I still also know By the good one may do

THE NEW HOME
STILL LEADS!

GUSTAV SEEGER,
170 Canal Street, 170
NEW ORLEANS, LA.

General dealer in all kinds of
SEWING MACHINES,
AND
Sewing Machine Supplies

The Highest Award!

THE GOLD MEDAL

—AWARDED TO THE—

LIGHT & RUNNING

New Home Sewing Machine

Above all Competitors at the late
Paris Exposition.

Call and examine the New Home
And you will buy no other.

DANTE. (Cantiléne.)

ments   que la ru meur   gran-dis-san - te   Dé ter-nels   res-sen - ti -
only   the ev- er increasing clam- or............ of   e - ternal..   quar - rel-

Allegro.

ments...............
ling...................

tempo tranquille.   *dim.*   pp

Mes fré - res, mes a - mis!........ Le
My broth - ers, my friends!......... The

ciel..... est si bleu sur Flo-ren - ce   Son   a - zur..... a tant de dou
heavens are so blue above Flo - rence....   Their   a - zure..... is so pure

Dante.

Cantiléne.

1

Andante molto.

Dante.

Piano.

Le ciel est si bleu sur Flo-ren-ce Son a-
The heavens are so blue a-bove Florence,...... Their a-

zur........ a tant de dou-ceurs Qu'un chant d'a-mour et d'es-pé-
zure....... is so pure........... That songs of love and hope.....

ran-ce De-vrait mon-ter, mon-ter de tous les coeurs; mais la
.... should a-rise......... from all...... hearts; but the

bri - se fré-mis-san-te....... N'em por-te aux clairs fir ma-
wav - ing breeze................. Carries towards the...... skies....

---

8 DANTE.

DANTE. *A part, comme un rêve.*
Pour être aimé
(*au peuple*) Je veux tenter l'œuvre suprême.
À vous mon bras et mon esprit,
(*regardant Béatrice*)   et mon cœur.
GEMMA.
Il l'aime, il l'aime encore.
BEATRICE.
Il m'aime.
Tous.
Salut au Maître. Salut au Protecteur.
CHEFS GIBELINS—*Montrant leur drapeau.*
Voici notre drapeau.
CHEFS GUELFES—*Designant leur bannière.*
C'est le nôtre.
Tous—*A Dante.* Lequel sera le tien.
DANTE.
(*Saisissant le gonfalon et le déployant.*)
Le drapeau de Florence.
Oui, ce peuple qui met en moi son espérance,
Ne doit plus voir que lui, flottant sous notre ciel.
(*On revêt Dante du riche manteau des Prieurs de Florence.*)

DANTE.
Plus de discorde criminelle,
Que nos vains débats soient finis;
Soyons à jamais réunis
Dans une étreinte fraternelle.
A notre voix, noble cité
Que ton front penché se relève.
Tous tes enfants n'ont qu'un seul rêve,
Ta grandeur et ta liberté
BEATRICE, BARDI, et Tous—*Reprenant.*
Plus de discorde, etc.
Salut, honneur, au Protecteur.

DANTE—*Aside, as in a dream.*
To be loved!
To the people) I will try the supreme task.
Yours is my arm, and my head and my heart.
Looking at Beatrice.
GEMMA.
He loves her, he loves her still.
BEATRICE.
He loves me...
CHORUS.
All hail to the master! Hail to the Protector.
GHIBELLINE CHIEFS—*Showing their banners.*
Here is our ensign.
GUELPH CHIEFS—*Showing theirs.*
Here is ours.
All (*to Dante*) which will be thine?
DANTE.
(*Grasping the gonfalon and displaying it.*)
The banner of Florence!
Yes, this people, which puts in it its hope,
Shall only see that, floating under our heaven.
Dante is invested with the rich mantle of the priors of Florence.

DANTE.
No more criminal discord.
Let our vain disputes be ended ;
Let us forever be united
In a fraternal embrace.
At our voice noble city
Let thy doomed front be redressed.
All thy children have a sole dream,
Thy greatness and thy freedom.
BEATRICE, BARDI, AND ALL.
No more discord, etc.,
Hail, honor to the Protector.

ACTE II.

[Le théâtre représente une salle du Palais des Seigneurs. Elle est éclairée par de grandes baies vitrées. Au fond un rideau de tapisserie. Portes à droite et à gauche. Vers la gauche, un grand fauteuil, près d'une table chargée de papiers. BARDI, seul en scène. Au lever du rideau il est assis dans le fauteuil et parcourt les papiers qui sont sur la table.]

SCÈNE 1.

BARDI.

Nos généreux espoirs seront-ils vains! Je tremble
A voir comme sur nous s'est assombri le ciel ;
Les chefs des deux partis qu'on a proscrits en-
[semble
Ensemble ont fait appel.
A Charles de Valois, frère du roi de France...
Il se lève.
Qu'on ouvre à l'étranger les portes de Florence.
O maître, c'en est fait d'un reste de pouvoir.
(*Il marche rêveur.*)

ACT II.

The theatre represents a hall in the palace of the noblemen. It is lighted by large bay windows. In the rear a tapestry curtain. Doors on the right and on the left. To the left a large arm chair near a table covered with papers. Bardi alone on the scene. When the curtain rises he is seated in the armchair and looks over the papers on the table.

SCENE 1.

BARDI.

Will our generous hopes be vain ! I tremble
To see how the sky has darkened over us.
The chiefs of the two parties who were proscrib-
[ed together
To Charles de Valois brother of the king of
(*He rises.*)   [France.
To open to the strangers the doors of Florence.
Oh masters! This ends the remains of our power.
(*He walks dreamily.*)

DANTE.

CHŒUR DU PEUPLE.
Le peuple a rendu sa sentence!
Salut à Dante Alighieri.

BEATRICE, *tressaille.*
Gemma, ce nom. Que disent-ils ?

GEMMA.
C'est Dante qu'on nomme!

CHŒUR.
Le peuple a rendu sa sentence.
Salut, honneur, gloire à Dante,
Salut, honneur, gloire au Prieur.
Dante paraît sur la place, Béatrice l'aperçoit.

BEATRICE.
Lui !
Bardi va au devant de Dante et l'amène sur la scène.

BARDI.
Venez écouter le peuple de Florence.

DANTE.
O peuple ! Que veux-tu de moi ?

CHŒUR.
En toi nous avons confiance.
Commande et nous suivrons ta loi.

DANTE.
Quoi ! vous voulez que je me jette
Dans la bataille et la tempête.
Au sein des partis furieux.
Non, Non,
Je ne sais, rêveur tranquille
Que m'en aller, lisant Virgile,
Par les sentiers emplis de chants mystérieux.

CHŒUR.
O Dante, sauve nous des partis furieux.

BARDI.
Entends ce peuple qui te prie,
Il met en toi tout son espoir ;
Florentin, défends ta patrie,
Pour être grand, fais ton devoir.

DANTE.
Ma force est inégale à la tâche imposée,
Et mon âme aujourd'hui,
Défaillante et brisée,
Plutôt que d'en prêter aurait besoin d'appui.

BARDI.
Entends ce peuple......etc.

CHŒUR.
En toi nous avons confiance......etc.
Béatrice sort lentement de la foule et s'avance vers Dante qui la contemple, muet et comme fasciné par son regard.

BEATRICE.
Quand ils vont aux dangers sans nombre,
Réclamés des peuples ravis,
Par d'autres cœurs cachés dans l'ombre,
. Les vaillants sont parfois suivis.
Ce doux cortège de tendresses
Autour de toi tu peux l'avoir.
Vas sans regrets, sois sans faiblesse.
Pour être aimé fais ton devoir.

CHORUS OF THE PEOPLE
The people has given its verdict.
Hail to Dante Alighieri!

BEATRICE.
(*trembling*) Gemma, whose name!
What are they saying ?

GEMMA.
It is Dante who is elected!

CHORUS.
The people has given its verdict.
Hail, honor, glory to Dante
Hail, honor, glory to the prior.
Dante appears on the square, Beatrice sees him.

BEATRICE.
He !
Bardi goes to meet Dante and leads him to the scene.

BARDI.
Hear the people of Florence.

DANTE.
Oh people ! What dost thou want of me ?

CHORUS.
In thee we have confidence.
Command and we will follow thy law.

DANTE.
What! you want that I should throw myself
Into the battle and the storm,
Into the bosom of the furious parties !
No! No!
I a quiet dreamer, who knows
Only to walk along, reading Virgil,
By the paths filled with mysterious melodies.

CHORUS
Oh Dante, save us from the furious parties, etc.

BARDI.
Hear this people which begs thee
It puts all its hope in thee.
Florentine, defend thy country.
To be great, perform thy duty.

DANTE.
My strength is unequal to the task imposed,
And my soul to-day,
Wavering and broken
Instead of giving, would require support.

BARDI.
Hear this people......etc.

CHORUS.
In thee we have confidence, etc.
Beatrice issues slowly from the crowd and advances towards Dante who contemplates her, silently and as fascinated by her look.

BEATRICE.
When they go to numberless dangers,
At the call of excited people,
By others heart, hidden in the shadow,
The valiant are sometimes followed.
This sweet cortege of tendernesses,
Around thee thou wilt have ; be without weak-
Go without regret ;   [uess.
To be loved, do thy duty !

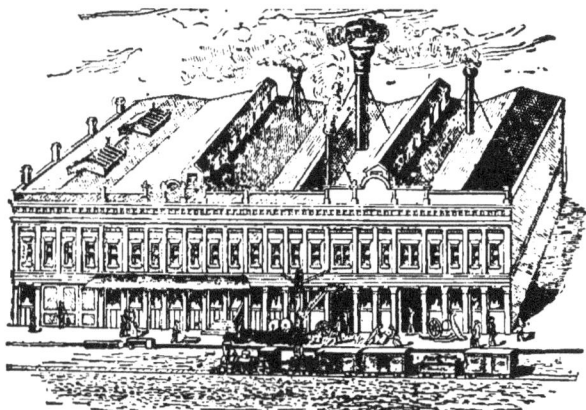

---

6   DANTE.

Tout est fini
Pour moi sur la terre
Hélas!
Mais non! Je ne veux pas désespérer encor!
Il faut que je la voie, il faut que je lui parle!
A m'entendre va tressaillir son cœur;
Ah! je saurai reprendre à qui l'osait ravir ce cœur,
Mon seul trésor!

Il sort vivement.

SCENE IV.

BEATRICE, GEMMA.

(Béatrice et Gemma sortent de la chapelle, Béatrice s'avance la première, la tête inclinée avec un air d'accablement profond.)

GEMMA.

Courage Béatrice,
Celui que nous venons de prier toutes deux
Saura te soutenir au jour du sacrifice.

BEATRICE.

Si le ciel exauçait mes vœux,
Lorsque viendra ce jour je franchirais ces portes
Avec le voile blanc qu'on met au front des mortes.

GEMMA.

Ah! tais-toi, c'est affreux!

BEATRICE.

Tu sais bien, chère confidente,
Que j'aimerai toujours celui qu'on nomme Ali-
Que moi j'appelais: Dante.   [ghieri,

GEMMA.

Que cet amour soit loin de toi comme de lui.

BEATRICE.

Il n'était qu'un enfant, j'étais toute petite
Lorsque je l'ai connu pour la première fois.
Sans doute plus heureux, il oublia plus vite....
Ce temps loin de son cœur, toujours je le revois!
Comme deux oiseaux que leur vol rassemble
Nous allions par le grand jardin
Sans savoir pourquoi, joyeux d'être ensemble.
Mais parfois aussi rougissant soudain,
Et puis je venais, sous les lauriers roses,
Près de lui m'asseoir afin d'écouter
Les récits charmants et les douces choses
Qu'il savait déjà si bien raconter.

ENSEMBLE.

BEATRICE.

Nous allions tous deux par le grand jardin, etc.

GEMMA.

Que cet amour soit loin de toi comme de lui.

Béatrice baisse le front; Gemma l'attire tendrement sur sa poitrine.

Ah! pleure librement, pleure, et de ta souffrance
Verse en mon âme le secret.
Qui donc, mieux que moi, hélas, la comprendrait!

SCENE V —Final.

BEATRICE, GEMMA, DANTE, BARDI, GUEL- FES ET GIBELINS.

Des clameurs sortent du Palais; de tous côtés sur la place arrivent des groupes animés.

All is finished
For me on earth
Alas! but no
I will not yet despair!
I must see her
I must speak to her!
Her heart will soften at hearing me.
Ah I shall know how to win back that heart
From the one who dared ravish it from me,
My only treasure!   (*He goes out rapidly.*)

SCENE IV

BEATRICE, GEMMA.

Beatrice and Gemma issue from the chapel. Beatrice approaches first, her head bowed, with an air of profound discouragement.

GEMMA.

Courage, Beatrice.
The one whom we both prayed just now
Will know how to sustain thee on the day of the   [sacrifice.

BEATRICE.

If heaven heard my prayer
When this day shall come I should issue from   [these gates
With the white shroud put on the dead.

GEMMA.

Ah! silence, this is awful!

BEATRICE.

Thou knowest well dear confident,
That I shall always love the one they call
Whom I called Dante,   [Alighieri.

GEMMA.

Let this love be far from thee, as from him.

BEATRICE.

He was but a child, I was quite small
When I first knew him.
Without doubt, being more happy, he forgot
       more quickly.
That time which is far from his heart.
I still forever see it.........
Like two birds united by their flight
We went through the great garden,
Without knowing why, joyous to be together,
But sometimes also suddenly blushing.
And then I used to come in the rosy laurels,
To sit near him so as to hear
His charming tales and the sweet things
He knew already so well how to tell.

TOGETHER.

BEATRICE.

We both went through the great garden....

GEMMA.

Let this love be far, etc.

Beatrice bows her head, Gemma draws her tenderly to her heart.

Ah! weep freely, weep in thy distress.
Pour into my heart thy secret,
Who better than me, alas, would understand it.

SCENE V.—Final.

BEATRICE, GEMMA, DANTE, BARDI, GUELPHS and GHIBELLINES.

Chorus are heard from the palace From all sides animated groups arrive on the square.

Celle que dès longtemps,
Et de toute mon âme
J'adorais en secret!

DANTE, *en souriant.*

Et la femme, il paraît,
En tous points est parfaite!

BARDI.

Pour bien la dépeindre, ô poëte,
C'est ton langage qu'il faudrait.
On ne saurait quelles choses
Lui comparer ici-bas;
Si Dieu n'avait fait les roses,
Si le lys n'existait pas!
Tant d'innocence et de grâce
Illumine ses quinze ans
Qu'on sourit quand elle passe
Comme on sourit aux enfants.
Et cependant auprès d'elle
On vient parfois à trembler
De la voir ouvrant son aile
Comme un ange s'envoler!

DANTE.

Dis-moi son nom!

BARDI.

Jadis vous deviez la connaître;
C'est la fille de maître Portinari.

DANTE, *à part avec douleur.*
Qu'ai-je entendu, Seigneur!
Beatrice. (*à Simeone.*) Ah! ce cœur
Comment l'as-tu gagné?

BARDI.

Par la reconnaissance :
A ce puissant parti qui règne sur Florence
Son père avait fait une offense,
Mais j'ai pu l'arracher aux mains des Donati.

DANTE, *avec amertume.*

L'enfant est le prix du service,
(*à part.*)   O Béatrice,
Pourquoi suis-je parti!

BARDI, *s'adressant à Dante en souriant.*

Mais en étant amant fidèle
On peut rester bon citoyen.
Pardonnez-moi, je vais où le devoir m'appelle.
*Il rentre au Palais Dante reste altéré sur le devant
de la Scène.*

DANTE, *avec désespoir.*

Ah! de tous mes espoirs il ne me reste plus rien!
En vain l'avenir rayonne,
Qu'importe un nom glorieux!
De quoi serai-je envieux
Quand mon amour m'abandonne!
(*avec accablement.*)   Tout est fini
Pour moi sur la terre!
Comme un banni
Je fuirai solitaire.
Par les chemins où je marchais vainqueur
Plus de bonheur,
D'ivresse promise :
Mon triste cœur
A jamais se brise!
Rêve menteur.
O tendresse éphémère.
Envoles-toi d'un éternel essor!

The one whom long
And with all my soul
I adored in secret!

DANTE—*Smiling.*

And the woman, it seems,
Is perfect in all points?

BARDI

To well depict her, oh, poet,
I should borrow your language
I would not know what things
Here below to compare her to,
If God had not made the roses,
If the lily did not exist!
So much innocence and race
Illuminates her fifteen years.
All smile when she passes
As one smiles to children.
And whoever approaches her
Sometimes tremble
To see her open her wings
To fly away like an angel!

DANTE.

Tell me her name!

BARDI.

Formerly you must have known her!
She is the daughter of master Portinari

DANTE—*Aside, with sorrow.*
What did I hear, Oh Lord.
Beatrice !....(*To Simeone*) Ah! this heart,
How didst thou win it?

BARDI.

Through gratitude :
To that powerful party, which reign over Florence
Her father had done some offense,
But I saved him from the hands of the Donati.

DANTE—*With bitterness.*

The child is the price of the service.
(*aside*)   Oh Beatrice!
Why did I depart!

BARDI—*Addressing Dante smiling.*

But while being a faithful lover
One may remain a good citizen
Pardon me. I go where duty calls me.
*He enters the palace. Dante remains sadly in
front of the scene.*

DANTE—*In despair.*

Ah! of all my hopes nothing remains.
In vain the future sparkles
What value a glorious name!
What have I to envy,
When my love forsakes me!
(*With despair*) All is finished
For me in this world,
Like one banished
I shall solitary fly
By the path I walked a victor
No more happiness,
Nor the promised bliss
My sad heart
Breaks forever!
Lying dream
Ephemeral tenderness,
Fly away with an eternal flight!

NEW ORLEANS
Brewing ✹ Association,

Office; 194 Common Street

NEW ORLEANS, LA.

———❖———

BOARD OF DIRECTORS

Peter Blaise,   Ph. W. Dielmann,   Theo. Brummer,   H. Lochte,
J. Langles,   Albt. P. Noll,   Geo. Fachule.

A. BRIFFOD,
Bakery and Confectionery,
427 DRYADES STREET.

TEA AND COFFEE STORE,

*Spices, French and American Choco-
late, Pies, Cakes, Fine Candy,
Soda Water.*

**Wedding Parties Orders attended to ON SHORT
NOTICE.**

Bread delivered twice a day.

☞Goods delivered free of charge to any part of the City.

4   DANTE.

N'emporte aux clairs firmaments
Quo la rumeur grandissante
D'éternels ressentiments......

*Les Chefs Guelfes et Gibelins accueillent ces paroles
avec des gestes de dédain et de colère, mais ceux qui
les entourent baissent la tête; quelques-uns remet-
tent leur épée au fourreau. Le peuple a entendu
les paroles de Dante avec émotion.*

CHŒUR DU PEUPLE.
Il a raison. Pourquoi donc tant de haine ?
Nous pourrions être heureux en nous tendant la
LES CHEFS GIBELINS.   [main
La politique est notre affaire,
Poëte passe ton chemin.

LES CHEFS GUELFES.
Écoute un avis tout contraire!
Un Prieur on va faire choix,
Mets-toi donc sur les rangs
Je te promets ma voix.

CHŒUR GENERAL.
Les collèges du Peuple au Palais se rassemblent.

CHEFS GUELFES.
Voyez comme ils ont peur.
Vainqueurs ce soir, maîtres demain.

CHEFS GIBELINS.
Regardez comme ils tremblent,
Vainqueurs ce soir, maîtres demain.

CHŒUR GENERAL.
Pourquoi donc tant de haine,
Nous pourrions être heureux, etc....
Tous entrent au Palais excepté Dante.

SCENE III.

DUO.

DANTE, BARDI.

DANTE.
Ah! puisse la voix populaire
Choisir pour l'œuvre tutélaire
Un homme qui la comprendra !
(Rêvant) Le fardeau sera lourd à qui l'acceptera.
*Simeone Bardi paraît. Il fait quelques pas dans la
direction du Palais, mais il voit Dante, s'approche
et le reconnaît.*

BARDI.
Vous! cher Dante, c'est vous.

DANTE.
Simeone.

BARDI.
Florence retrouve enfin
Après si longue absence,
Son fils très oublieux......
Pourtant très regretté.

DANTE.
A Bologne.... à Padoue....
Et dans toute cité
Dont j'allais consultant l'histoire et le génie,
Jamais de la terre bénie,
Le souvenir ne m'a quitté.

BARDI, *avec expansion.*
J'aurai donc pour témoin de ma félicité
L'ami de ma jeunesse.
Dante l'interroge du geste et du regard.
On me donne pour femme

Carries to the clear firmament
But the swelling rumor
Of eternal resentments.

*The Guelphs and Ghibelline chiefs receive these words
with signs of disdain, but those surrounding them
bow their head ; some sheathe their words. The
people have heard the words of Dante with emo-
tion.*

CHORUS of the PEOPLE.
He is right. Why then so much hate!
We might be happy did we join hands
THE GHIBELLINE CHIEFS
Politics are our affair.
Poet, go your way.

THE GUELPH CHIEFS.
Hear a quite contrary advice
A prior is to be chosen,
Enter then the list,
I promise thee my vote.

GENERAL CHORUS.
The colleges of the people are assembling at the
GUELPH CHIEFS.   [palace.
See how they are afraid.
Victor this evening, masters to-morrow.

GHIBELLINE CHIEFS.
Look how they tremble,
Victors this evening, masters to-morrow.

GENERAL CHORUS.
Why then so much, etc.
All enter the palace except Dante.

SCENE III.

DUO.

DANTE—BARDI.

DANTE.
Ah! may the popular voice
Choose for the protecting work
A man who will understand it !
(Dreaming) The task will be heavy, for whoever
  [may accept it.
*Simeone Bardi appears. He advance towards the
palace, but sees Dante, approaches and recognizes
him*

BARDI.
You! Dear Dante, it is you ?
DANTE.
Simeone !

BARDI.
Florence at last finds again,
After so long an absence,
Her very forgetful son,
Who is nevertheless much regretted.

DANTE.
At Bologna   at Padua,
And in all cities
Of which I consulted the history and the genius.
The sacred remembrance of my country has not
  [left me.

BARDI—*With expression.*
I shall then have as a witness of my felicity.
The friend of my youth.
    (Dante looks askance at him.)
I am soon to wed

DANTE.

ACTE I.	ACT I.
SCENE I.	SCENE I.

Le théâtre représente la place publique à Floren-co. Au fond le palais du gouvernement. A droite l'entrée d'une chapelle. Au lever du rideau, deux groupes de Guelfes et de Gibelins conduits, l'un par Corso et l'autre par Vieri se défient et se menacent. Derrière eux et de chaque côté groupes de gens du peuple.

CHŒUR DES GIBELINS et CHŒUR DES GUELFES.
alternativement

> Malheur à vous dont l'audace
> Nous insulte et nous menace
> Ah! votre pouvoir s'efface
> C'est votre dernier effort!
> A nous fortune et puissance,
> A vous l'exil et la mort.
> Quand la ville de Florence
> Aura dicté sa sentence
> A vous l'exil, à vous la mort
> Malheur à vous! à vous la mort.

LES CHEFS GIBELINS.
> Aux amis de César la victoire est promise,
> O Guelfes nous avons avec nous l'Empereur.

LES CHEFS GUELFES.
> Le Ciel est favorable aux amis de l'Eglise.
> Gibelins, le Saint-Siège est notre protecteur.

LES CHEFS GIBELINS.
> Quand Florence aujourd'hui va nommer le Prieur,
> Le Gonfalonier de justice
> Pensez-vous qu'elle choisisse
> Ailleurs que dans notre parti ?

LES CHEFS GUELFES.
> Le Prieur sortira des rangs des Donati.

ENSEMBLE.
> Malheur à vous dont, etc.

SCENE II.
Récit et Cantilène.

DANTE, LES PRECEDENTS.

DANTE.
> Guelfes ou Gibelins, qu'importe la bannière,
> Blancs ou noirs, fils ingrats, vous frappez votre
> [mère,
> La Patrie est en deuil lorsque vous combattez.

CHŒUR GENERAL.
> C'est Dante Alighieri, c'est le maître, écoutez!

DANTE.
> Mes frères, mes amis, qu'elle est votre démence?
> Le ciel est si bleu sur Florence
> Son azur a tant de douceurs
> Qu'un chant d'amour et d'espérance
> Devrait monter de tous les cœurs.
> Mais la brise frémissante

The theatre represents the Public Square at Florence. In the rear the Government palace. When the curtain rises two groups of Guelphs and Ghibellines, led one by Corso and the other by Vieri dare and threaten each other. Behind them and on each side groups of the people.

CHORUS of GHIBELLINES and Chorus of GUELPHS
alternately

> Death to you whom daring
> Insults and menaces us
> Ah! your power vanishes
> This is your last effort!
> Fortune and power are ours
> For you exile and death.
> When the City of Florence
> Shall have dictated the sentence
> For you exile and death,
> Death to you, death to you.

THE GUELPH CHIEFS.
> To the friends of Corso victory is promised,
> Oh, Guelphs, we have with us the Emperor.

THE GUELPH CHIEFS.
> Heaven is propitious to the friends of the Church
> Ghibellines! The Holy See is our protector.

THE GHIBELLINE CHIEFS.
> When Florence, to-day, names the prior,
> The Gonfalonier of justice.
> Do you think she will choose
> Outside of our party ?

THE GUELPH CHIEFS.
> The prior comes from the ranks of the Donati.

TOGETHER.
> Death to you whom, etc.

SCENE II.
Recit and Cantilene.

DANTE, *the same.*

DANTE:
> Guelphs or Ghibelines what matter the banner,
> White or black, ingrate sons, you strike your
> [mother
> The country is in danger when you combat.

GENERAL CHORUS.
> It is Dante Alighieri, it is the master here.

DANTE.
> My brothers, my friends are you demented
> Heaven is so blue over Florence
> Its azure is so sweet
> That a song of love and hope
> Should arise from all hearts
> But the trembling breeze

DANTE.

The Scene of this Opera is laid in Florence about the year 1300.
Two factions divide the City of Florence and fight for its
Government, the Guelfes and the Gibelins.

ACT I.

Opens on a public place in Florence. In the distance the Government's palace. On the right the entrance to a church. Groups of Guelfes and Gibelins led, the formers by Corso, the latter by Vieri threaten and defy one another. They are surrounded by men and women of the people. The day is that of the election of the Chief Magistrate of the City, and both parties are confident of their success. Enters Dante who reproaches them with their incessant quarrels and begs them, instead, unite their efforts against the enemies of their country. Guelfs and Gibelins laugh at him, but the people listen and advises Dante to present himself as a candidate at the election. They all enter the palace except Dante. Dante then meets Simeone Bardi, an old friend of his, who reproaches him for his long absence and informs him that he is betrothed to a lovely maiden, whose charms he exalts so much that Dante's curiosity is awakened, he asks Bardi who she is and learns that she is Beatrice Portanini, whom her father has promised him for a signalled service rendered, whom he loves and by whom he knew he was loved before he left Florence. Dante gives way to despair and leaves the scene. Enters Beatrice and Gemma her friend. Beatrice confesses to Gemma that she has always loved Dante and would rather die than be married to Bardi. She has scarcely uttered these words, when the people return from the palace and shout the name of Dante who has been elected Prior of the City. Dante appears brought back by Bardi and is seen by Beatrice. The poet refuses the honor proferred but Beatrice appeals to him and tells him that it is his duty to devote himself to his country and that he will find his reward in love. Dante understands that Beatrice loves him yet, he accepts the dignity of Grand Prior, and after exhorting the Florentines to cease their quarrels and unite against their enemies, and he is vested with the rich mantel of the Prior of Florence.

A. M. & J. SOLARI,

Cor. Royal and Customhouse Streets,

—— IMPORTERS OF ——

Choice Family Groceries,

—(:o:) WINES AND LIQUORS (:o:)——

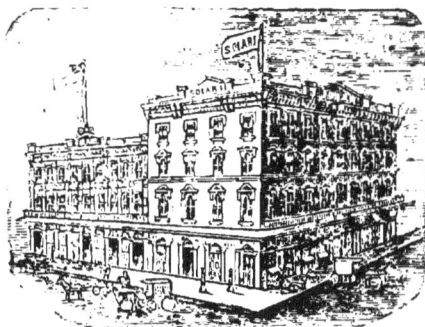

L. Roederer--Champagne { Carte Blanche, Rich and Fruity, Grand Vin Sec, Very Dry.

J. L. Duret & Co.--Olive Oil
This Oil is Warranted Pure and of Very Best Quality.

Before making purchases, please call and EXAMINE OUR STOCK and you will be CONVINCED that it is the

FINEST AND LARGEST
IN THE SOUTH.
And at Reasonable Prices.
All Goods are Warranted. No Charge for Packing nor Cartage.

P. J. MAGUIRE, *President.*   W. H BOFINGER, *Treasurer.*   WALTER L. SAXON *Chairman Finance Com.*

ALBERT MACKIE, *Vice President*   W. W HUCK. *Secretary.*   GEN. J. B VINET, *Chairman Real Estate Com.*

EUREKA
Homestead Society,

186 GRAVIER STREET.

Shares $500, payable $2,50 monthly.

This Society (established January 1, 1885,) is a purely local organization, is strictly mutual and co-operative, and possesses every progressive and liberal feature consistent with absolute security.

The EUREKA HOMESTEAD SOCIETY has no superiors; its prompt and equitable methods, its eminent success, its established reputation for security and profitable investment, make it preferable equally to borrowers and investors.

AUTHORIZED CAPITAL 50,000,000.   SHARES $100 EACH.

NEW SOUTH

Building and Loan Association

— OF —

NEW ORLEANS, LA.

—— ◦⊹◦ ——

Board of Directors.

HENRY GARDES.......................President American National Bank.
GEORGE R. PRESTON...... ....President Hibernia National Bank.
STANLEY O. THOMAS ...:...... .....President Citizens' Bank of Louisiana.
JOS A. SHAKS'EARE......................Mayor City of New Orleans.
HENRY GINDER........................ ....of A. B. Griswold & Co.
JAMES S. RICHARDSON............................of Richardson & May.
JULES A BLANC...... , ...Capitalist.
J. M. LEWIS, of Talladega, Ala................................ Capitalist.
JOHN HANSON KENNARD...... ....Attorney-at Law.
E. H. POWER

OFFICERS.

HENRY GARDES -   -   -   -   -   -   - President
JOS. A. SHAKSPEARE   -   -   -   - Vice-President
JULES A. BLAND   -   -   -   -   -   - Treasurer
HENRY GINDER   -   -   -   -   -   - Secretary
JOHN HANSON KENNARD   -   - General Attorney
E. H. POWER   -   -   -   -   - General Manager

A thoroughly solid and well managed Co-operative Association,
which offers unsurpassed advantages for the investment of money, as
also for loaning money at unusually low rates of interest, and for li-
quidation of same by easy monthly payments.

For information write to, or call at the Association's Office.

46 Camp Street, Corner of Gravier,

NEW ORLEANS, LA.

Address " New South Building and Loan Association."

French Opera Libretto and Commercial Guide

Season of 1890-91.

CATALOGUE OF OPERAS TO BE PUBLISHED.

Jewess.

Faust.

Huguenots.

La Traviata.

Favorite.

Carmen.

Prophet.

William Tell.

Lucie de Lammermoor.

Aida.

Gillette de Narbonne. 1st time in this City

La Muette de Portici.

Robert the Devil.

Roland à Roncevaux.

Le Dante, 1st time in this City.

Patrie, 1st time in this City.

La Cigale et la Fourmi, 1st time in this City.

Mignon.

Jerusalem.

Il Trovatore.

Romeo et Juliette.

L'Africaine.

Hamlet.

Rigoletto.

Mirelle, 1st time in this City.

PERSONNAGES.	CHARACTERS.
Dante Alighieri, le Poëte Florentin.	Dante Alighieri, the Florentine poet.
Béatrice Portarini, fiancée à Bardi.	Beatrice Portarini, engaged to Bardi.
Gemma, confidente de Béatrice.	Gemma, confident of Beatrice.
Simeone Bardi, gentilhomme Florentin.	Simeone Bardi, Florentine nobleman.
Vieri, gentilhomme Florentin.	Vieri, Florentine nobleman.
Chefs Guelfes et Gibelins.	Guelfs and Ghibelline chiefs.
Hommes et Femmes du Peuple. Ecoliers. Religieuses, etc.	Men and women of the people, students, nuns, etc.
PERSONNAGES DU REVE.	PERSONS OF THE DREAM.
Dante.	Dante.
L'ombre de Virgile.	The Shade of Virgil.
Apparitions { Ugolin. / Paolo et Francesca. / Anges. / Damnés.	Spirits—Ugolin. / Paolo. / Angels. / Damned.

Le 1er et 2e actes se passent à Florence.
Le 3e acte au tombeau de Virgile.
Le 4e acte dans un Convent de Naples.

The 1st and 2nd acts are located at Florence.
The 3rd act at the grave of Virgil.
The 4th act in a convent of Naples.

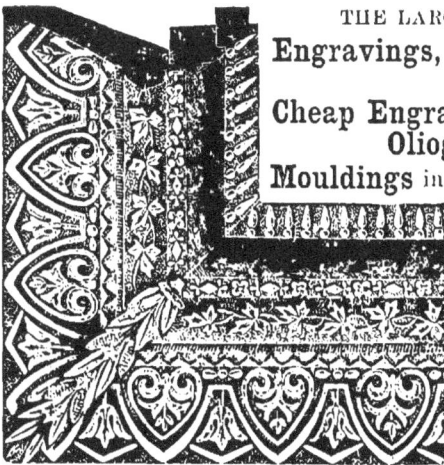

MASTERPIECES

:)OF THE(:

FRENCH ✸ OPERA.

Illustrated and Musical.

DANTE.

Lyrical Drama in 4 acts.

Text by Edouard Blau.   Music by Benjamin Godard.

First represented at the Opera Comique, Paris, in 1888. Deals with the war between Guelfs and Ghibelins, and makes Dante a young an. active participant.

Benjamin Godard whose Dante, is the first work ever presented before an american public, was born in Paris, August 18, 1849, and is still ving.

Mr. B Godard besides being one of the most noteworthy representatives g the young french composers, of the tendency inaugurated by Berlioz, is also tinguished violinist and a pupil of Vieuxtemps.

MASTERPIECES
—or—
FRENCH OPERAS.

DANTE

Opera in 4 Acts.

WORDS BY

EDOUARD BLAU.

MUSIC BY

Benjamin Godard.

Benjamin Godard, Edouard Blau

Dante

Lyrical drama in 4 acts

ISBN/EAN: 9783744794060

Printed in Europe, USA, Canada, Australia, Japan

Cover: Foto ©Thomas Meinert / pixelio.de

More available books at **www.hansebooks.com**

www.ingramcontent.com/pod-product-compliance
Lightning Source LLC
Chambersburg PA
CBHW022144090426
42742CB00010B/1388